FOREWORD BY
WILLIAM VANDERBLOEMEN

THE SUPPORTING CAST

A GUIDE FOR CHURCH STAFF

ANTHONY C. COBBS, ED.D

GC2
PRESS

The Supporting Cast: A Guide for Church Staff

GC2 Press® Leadership Team:
Executive Director, BGCT: Julio Guarneri
Associate Executive Director, BGCT: Craig Christina
Treasurer/CFO, BGCT: Ward Hayes
Director, Center for Church Health, BGCT: Phil Miller
Interim Publisher, GC2 Press®: Stan Granberry
Production, Design, and Printing: D6 Family Ministry
                    Summit Digital Media, LLC

Ordering Information: www.GC2Press.org

First Edition: April 2025
ISBN-978-1-961120-14-3

DEDICATION

This book is dedicated to the many servants of Christ
I have had the privilege of recruiting, training, supervising
and mentoring. You have made me a better leader
and I pray in some way I have added to your life.
You are amazing!

TABLE OF CONTENTS

FOREWORD

How do I find the work I'm wired to do?

Lots of people ask this question either out loud, or subconsciously. But we aren't finding the answer. Nearly two thirds of all Americans hate their job. They're not "mildly dissatisfied," or "disengaged." They hate their jobs. My experience and study tell me that number isn't as high in pastoral ministry, but it's still high. Why? Church work is hard. I don't know a single occupation that will occupy as much of life as pastoral ministry. You do work at work. You do church at work. Your friends are at work. The people who don't like you "at work" can functionally make life pretty miserable. And then there are the good parts. Nothing beats seeing a life change and turn around. As a pastor and client once told me, "William, ministry is the most brutiful job in the world."

It's just that. Brutal. Beautiful. And all consuming, brutiful.

That's why it's so important that people in ministry find the very best niche in ministry for their wiring and calling. And it's why I'm excited to introduce you to Anthony Cobbs' new book. You're holding a resource in your hands that will help you find that niche. I wish I would have had this book when I started pastoral ministry. It gives a clear path to determining where you might best fit in ministry.

Life is too short to hate your job. And work is too many hours to hate your job. Let's start a journey with Anthony. Let's learn how

God has you wired and discover the work God has specifically called you to do. It will help you be happier at your job, and it will help you be more fruitful for Jesus.

William Vanderbloemen Founder and CEO Vanderbloemen
https://vanderbloemen.com

INTRODUCTION

JOINING THE SUPPORTING CAST

Carlie entered her interview for the role of Children's Director practically glowing. The committee loved her—the energy, the ideas, the pure joy she radiated at the thought of working with children in a ministry context. Frankly, I could see them all imagining her in that role and taking our children's ministry to new heights. But as excited as everyone else was, I felt a hesitation I couldn't quite shake. It wasn't because Carlie lacked any skills; she was clearly gifted. My concern was for her spirit, the light in her eyes, exuding enthusiasm and joy. I worried that might not survive the life of a church staff member.

Two years later, that light had gone out. The energy and joy that once defined her seemed to have faded. She was drained, worn thin by the demands of ministry, and wrestling with the kind of church life she hadn't anticipated. Carlie served up a somber warning about what can easily happen when workers in church staff positions pour out their lives sacrificially. Serving in a church is rewarding, but it can also be exhausting and depleting. A number of recent studies have attempted to quantify and qualify this phenomenon, and they indicate that staff serving in pastoral or non-pastoral positions are experiencing a similar kind of burned-out, loss-of-joy kind of existence.

According to a recent Vanderbloemen Search Group report, staff members in non-pastoral positions typically serve about four to six years in their roles and struggle with chronic challenges related to work-life balance, feeling demanded in ways that seem unreasonable and unhealthy.

This book aims to assist those contemplating a church ministry role in avoiding burnout and maintaining their shine, even in the arduous environment that can be church work. For 25 years, I've served on church staff, including two decades in executive and lead pastor roles. The privilege of working alongside incredible people with unique strengths and unfailing passions has largely characterized my ministry. Yet, I know firsthand the toll that ministry can take on someone, not just on their profession but also on their health and relationships—if they go into it without a clear sense of purpose and who knows what else. With more and more people going into ministry, or wanting to, a number of them will need to know ways to withstand the rigors of the calling and come out on the other side healthy and re-energized.

In this book, I distill the wisdom gained from my journey so far and offer practical advice and encouragement for not just surviving but thriving on church staff. I tackle everything from understanding your part in the drama of church life, to managing life (both personal and professional) when you're on staff, to knowing when (and how) to move on if your church calling comes to an end. I truly hope you'll not only serve your church well but also find ways to keep your light fully shining for years to come.

At the end of each chapter, you'll find what I call "Mentor Moments." These are conversation guides intended to foster meaningful dialogue between new staff members and their supervisors or mentors. My hope is that these guides will be a valuable resource for pastors, executive or assistant pastors, and human resource professionals as they support and develop their ministry teams.

Let's delve into what it signifies to be part of the behind-the-scenes team, contributing to something that stretches beyond our individual selves and makes an impact that, with God's grace, will last for eternity.

CHAPTER 1

FINDING THE RIGHT ROLE

Before you take on a church staff role, you must ask yourself: Am I the person to fill this role? Working on church staff is unlike any other job. Working on church staff is like being in a supporting role in a play or film. Your job is to lift up the church's mission, keep it going, and make sure it doesn't miss a beat, all without stealing the spotlight. And all the while, you're performing for an audience of One.

During my years in ministry, I've seen a lot of people come and go. I've seen some folks do really well. They were born to serve in the church. They have gifts and a calling that are tailor- made for working with (or as) a church staff member. I've seen some folks do really poorly.

They are not serving properly, nor are they being served properly.

Church staff is a demanding environment, and the kinds of people who are tempted to burn out first are too often the same types of folks who can't figure out what role they play and don't understand the mission of the church.

In ministry, all the difference comes from feeling "called" to the work. At first glance, working for the church may seem like a typical job, one that offers a measure of satisfaction and a secure paycheck in easy times, plus the opportunity to do good and make positive changes, all while "working for God." But make no mistake: working for the church is also a life of service, or servitude, in which you are told to put the needs of others and the church above your own.

The Bible is replete with examples of people who were placed into or took on roles of leadership because they were convinced, they were "called" by God to serve. Moses is the poster child for being called to do a great work. Elijah, Jonah, and the prophets are other examples of being recruited to do God's will. Esther stepped up for her people when she was needed, the disciples left all to follow a man named Jesus and changed the world as a result. The list goes on and on and continues with those who are called to church staff.

THE THREE-FOLD ROLE OF CHURCH STAFF

Taking on a church staff position means balancing three roles simultaneously. Even though your title and job description might suggest a singular focus, really, you're stepping into three roles: church member, staff member, and member of God's kingdom.

Church Member: In many churches, you might be expected to also be a member of the church. Even if it is not required for the job; your presence and example make you part of a family of faith. This connection is vital. Every church staff member must model for the congregation the kind of commitment that is life-changing and leads to the kind of servanthood that Christ exemplified. You must show that you are in it for the long haul, living out your faith in every facet of your life, as the church community watches and sometimes critiques from the sidelines.

Staff Member: The second role you occupy is that of church staff member (or leader). When you accepted this position, you signed up for a job that has job-like responsibilities. You must not use working at a church as a reason to slack but instead as a motivator to excel. And sometimes, that's no fun, but that's what makes you a leader. You have duties and expectations that you are there to fulfill. You are accountable to the church and the team you work with, and there are consequences when those expectations are not met.

Kingdom Member: If you are a believer who has placed their faith in God through His son Jesus Christ, you are a part of the kingdom of God. As a believing church staff member, you are an ambassador who models before others the right kind of decisions that lead to kingdom growth—decisions that serve to remind them that what happens in this life directly impacts their experience in the next life.

Note: If you are reading this and unsure of what you believe or what any of this talk about God and Jesus means, please see your pastor or another church leader to get information about Jesus and His love for you.

IDENTIFYING THE APPROPRIATE PLACE FOR YOUR TALENTS AND INTERESTS

Once you grasp the nature of the different church staff roles, the next task is to determine if a potential ministry position fits with your skill set and strengths. Some callings don't require church staff to fulfill them, and not every role in a church is meant for every person. When you find the right fit, the level of serving you achieve is unprecedented, both in your life and in the church you're serving.

Are You Suited for This Role?

Every person has different gifts to serve in the body of Christ. Some folks are more on the organizing side, and some are more on the teaching side. Some people are extraordinary "behind-the-scenes" folks—like architects and engineers—while others are much better front-and-center types, like public speakers. Whoever you are and whatever you're good at, the church needs you and your abilities. When it comes to staff positions, different churches have different needs.

How Can You Meet the Ministry Life Head-On?

Ministry can be more than a calling; it can be a life half lived if you are not well-suited and well- prepared for the demands that come with the role. Research and experience from organizations like Vanderbloemen Search Group reveal far too many pastors and church staff are not practicing the resiliency needed to withstand the twisting and turning paths of this vocation. We see many not mentalizing the grit needed to maintain their emotional health and maturity over the long haul. We also see too many church leaders who are not maintaining their physical health.

Is the Church's Mission and Culture a Good Fit for You?

Each church has a different mission and culture, often defined by their history, leadership, and the nature of their congregational needs. If a church's mission resonates with your own values and calls, working there—however you might serve—can feel really meaningful. If not, if you find the church's already established mission doesn't speak to your heart, it can be tough to get up and go to work. Or, in the case of this kind of cross-cultural mission work, it can be tough to get on a plane bound for wherever you're going next.

Will You Grow and Change?

Church staff can often count on one thing: change. And if you plan on serving in ministry, get used to the notion that you're probably going to be asked to do something completely different with your skill set pretty regularly. You might be leading a team today and next week be asked to receive direction as a team member. Hang on to your hat; it's a wild ride. The good news is that it can be fulfilling and really fun if you give yourself the freedom to try things on for size, learn a lot along the way, and, as always, keep the end goal in mind: serving your community and making the Jesus way of life an everyday reality for someone other than you.

SERVICE AND GROWTH: A PERSPECTIVE FROM THE CHURCH

Working on a church staff is not simply a secular employ. It's an opportunity to participate in a divine narrative that endows with meaning not merely a single life but also the lives of a congregation. Why? Because it is the very nature of ministry to give expression to what life can be when one lives under the reign of God. Ministry makes distinctly visible what makes the church the church and what makes a life with God a life worth living. To pursue a ministerial path is to embark upon a journey that travels outward along two vectors. One vector extends toward the light; the other vector extends toward love. To understand and appreciate the light, you have to know the source of the light.

The forthcoming chapter will engage with the process of locating one's unique position within the ecclesiastical body and appraising it for the sake of finding the specific, high-value role one might serve within the church. It is akin to tracing out the particular constellation one forms with the cast of church characters, a kind of selfie morphology. Each church staff role has some kind of electric charge it brings up a notch on the ministry's overall voltmeter. Together, we will find the right electric continuum for you in God's unfolding story.

REFLECTION QUESTIONS

1. What inspires you to seek a position on the church staff?

2. In what ways are you uniquely qualified to fulfill the distinctive responsibilities that come with being a church staff member?

3. How do you see yourself multiplying the impact of your church down here in the valley while also maintaining balance up there in the heavenly places?

MENTOR MOMENTS FOR CHAPTER 1
FINDING THE RIGHT ROLE

Objective—Guide the new staff member in exploring their motivations, calling, and readiness for church ministry, helping them understand what it means to be both a servant and a professional in this unique environment.

Session Title—Finding Your Fit: Embracing the Call to Serve

Time Required—30–45 minutes

REFLECTING ON CALLING AND PURPOSE

- **Mentor's Prompt**—"Church ministry is more than a job; it's a calling. As you step into this role, let's reflect on what brought you here and how you feel led by God to serve."

- **Questions for Reflection**
  - What specific reasons or experiences drew you to serve on church staff?
  - How do you sense God leading you in this role, and what is your motivation to serve?

NOTES

BALANCING THE THREEFOLD ROLE: CHURCH MEMBER, STAFF MEMBER, AND KINGDOM WORKER

- **Mentor's Guidance**—"As a church staff member, you'll find yourself in multiple roles—serving as a church member, a team member, and a representative of God's kingdom. Let's discuss how you'll navigate each one."

- **Questions to Consider**
  - How do you plan to maintain your spiritual growth and involvement as a church member?
  - What practices will help you balance personal faith with professional responsibilities?

NOTES

ALIGNING STRENGTHS WITH SERVICE

- **Mentor's Insight**—"God has uniquely equipped you with strengths and skills. Let's discuss how these align with the needs of this role and how they can enhance your ministry work."

- **Questions to Reflect On**
  - Which personal strengths do you feel are most aligned with this role?
  - In what areas do you anticipate needing support or growth?

NOTES

FINAL REFLECTION AND PRAYER

- **Mentor's Closing Thought**—"Take time to consider how you can serve faithfully and joyfully. Pray for God's guidance as you commit to this new role, asking Him to use you to make a meaningful impact."

- **Closing Prayer**—"Lord, thank You for guiding [staff member's name] into this calling. Help them to embrace this role with humility, dedication, and joy. May they honor You in all they do, and may their service bring glory to Your name. In Jesus' name, Amen."

CHAPTER 2

DISCOVERING YOUR PLACE IN THE BIGGER PICTURE

To be part of a church staff team means finding where your unique gifts, talents, and strengths align with the mission of the church. The ministry roles you and I occupy may differ, but each of us brings something unique and special to the execution of the church's work.

To understand this larger context and where you fit in takes some self-awareness, some introspection, and of course, the guidance of God's spirit.

In my years of working on church staff and serving as a Gallup-certified Strengths coach, I've seen how powerful it is for people to know and use their strengths. Knowing your strengths helps you lean into what you're naturally gifted at, enabling you to serve in a way that feels authentic and sustainable. While we all have areas we can improve, I believe in focusing on strengths rather than weaknesses. In this chapter, we'll explore how to discover your spiritual gifts, natural talents, and strengths so you can find a role that aligns with who God has made you to be.

UNCOVERING YOUR SPIRITUAL GIFTS

The church has many members, and each one has a place within it. To understand your place in the church is to understand your spiritual gifts. These gifts, given by God, are special abilities used to help and encourage people within the church. The apostle Paul talks about them with an exuberance that cannot be missed. To Paul, the gifts of the Spirit were important; they still are important to the life of the church. And they are important to you because if you understand your gifts, you begin to understand your way within the church.

In 1 Corinthians 12:4–7, Paul explained how the Spirit gives these gifts out. Paul went on to talk about the significance of the gifts and the importance of using them within the church. The exciting thing is these gifts are alive in you. God has blessed you with abilities to use in the life of the church.

ASSESSING YOUR SPIRITUAL GIFTS

A spiritual gifts assessment can provide a beneficial starting point for unearthing your gifts. This assessment often begins with a series of questions that help reveal the tendencies, strengths, and interests you have that correspond to potential spiritual gifts. As you attempt to ascertain your spiritual gifts, it is important not to rush the process and to remain open to the leading of the Holy Spirit. The gifts God has given you may not be immediately evident, and you may find that certain gifts are not always obvious during specific seasons of your life.

Remember, too, that even as you reflect on the results of the assessment, you should also be praying for discernment about how to live out any gifts that may have surfaced. In the next few paragraphs, we will look at some of the commonly held spiritual gifts and offer some potential signs that may indicate you have them. Again, these are not exhaustive or authoritative descriptions; they are simply guidelines.

INSTRUMENTS FOR UNEARTHING YOUR PRESENTS, ABILITIES, AND ADVANTAGES

When you think about your part in the church, make it a priority to figure out every aspect of what makes you unique, ranging from the gifts of the Spirit to what you may consider a natural talent (even if you've never thought of it that way before). Here are three excellent tools that can help you understand, on a deeper level, how the unique combination of what you've been given equips you to serve in your church:

Spiritual Gifts Assessment. An assessment of your spiritual gifts can help you pinpoint which not-so-apparent (Latin for "not-so-well-known") gifts the Holy Spirit has given you to carry out His work. Knowing which way they lean can give you a better idea of which direction you might take to follow the call of the Holy Spirit in your life.

The Gallup Strengths Finder is something I often urge people to take when I work with them as a coach. With an ample amount of research backing it, the *Strengths Finder* is a powerful tool that identifies the top five (or, for some, 34) strengths a person possesses. But unlike many other assessments, the Strengths Finder does not delve into personality types or how you are wired to be who you are (although this is probably very important to know, too). What the Strengths Finder does (and does very well) is identify the unique patterns of thought, feeling, and action that you inherently possess and that lead you toward high performance.

The DISC Personality Inventory is an assessment that classifies people into four basic styles: Dominance, Influence, Steadiness, and Conscientiousness. When you understand your DISC style, you understand why you prefer to communicate the way you do and why you interact with others the way you do. DISC really shines in ministry settings, where collaboration and teamwork are essential. When you and your fellow staff members understand your types, you can work together in more or less harmonious ways, with the understanding that you might express something like "staff love" (Acts 4:32) more as a Dominant staffer than as a softer, Steady type.

Each one of these assessments provides a 360-degree view of your abilities and affinities. Your spiritual gifts offer one kind of perspective on what you're good at and what's right for you.

Your strengths provide another. And when you consider all three together—gifts, strengths, and personality assessments—you begin to get an even better glimpse of what makes you tick and what kind of work you're well-suited for. These views of your hardwiring and soft wiring should be good indicators as to who you are and what's next for you.

When you comprehend your spiritual gifts, talents, and strengths, you can serve in ways that are authentic and fulfilling, helping you make a meaningful difference in your church. You have gifts that God wants you to use, and you have the right to that claim. You have also been given freedom in the Church to serve in ways that bring God glory and that resonate with you and your unique style.

REFLECTION QUESTIONS

1. Have you set aside time to evaluate your own strengths, personal traits, and spiritual gifts with the help of tools like the Gallup Strengths Finder, DISC, and a Spiritual Gifts Assessment?

2. How well do you understand your own "wiring," and how does it help you know where you fit on the church staff team?

3. How can you use your ways of being and doing to collaborate more effectively with your fellow staff members and increase the probability of the church's mission?

MENTOR MOMENTS FOR CHAPTER 2 DISCOVERING YOUR PLACE IN THE BIGGER PICTURE

Objective—Help the new staff member identify their unique role within the church, explore their spiritual gifts, and understand how their contributions align with the church's mission.

Session Title—Discovering Your Unique Role in the Body of Christ

Time Required—30–45 minutes

RECOGNIZING YOUR ROLE IN THE CHURCH BODY

- **Mentor's Prompt**—"Each role in the church is vital to the whole body. Let's talk about how you see your place within the church and how you feel your role supports the bigger mission."

- **Questions to Consider**

  ° How do you feel your role contributes to the mission of the church?

  ° In what ways do you feel called to support the church's vision?

NOTES

EXPLORING YOUR SPIRITUAL GIFTS

- **Mentor's Insight**—"Spiritual gifts are essential to understanding how we can serve best. Let's take some time to reflect on the gifts you feel God has given you and how they might shape your work in this role."
- **Reflection Questions**
  - Which spiritual gifts do you feel called to use in this position?
  - Is there a gift or skill you sense God is developing in you during this season?

NOTES

MATCHING PERSONAL STRENGTHS WITH MINISTRY NEEDS

- **Mentor's Guidance**—"Your unique strengths and talents are valuable assets to the team. Let's discuss how you see these abilities aligning with your new role."
- **Discussion Points**
  - How do you think your personal strengths will contribute to the specific needs of this role?
  - What areas do you hope to grow in as you serve?

NOTES

FINAL REFLECTION AND PRAYER

- **Mentor's Closing Thought**—"Take a moment to reflect on your unique calling in this ministry and pray that God will continue to reveal His purpose for you here."

- **Closing Prayer**—"Lord, thank You for placing [staff member's name] within this church body. May their gifts and strengths bring unity, love, and growth to our ministry. Guide them in serving joyfully and purposefully. In Jesus' name, Amen."

CHAPTER 3

QUESTIONS TO ASK BEFORE ACCEPTING A STAFF ROLE

When you're interviewing for a position on church staff, it's easy to concentrate solely on whether you're qualified for the role and whether the church is enthusiastic about bringing you on. But equally, if not more important is determining whether the church is suitable for you.

Ministry is about so much more than just doing a job well; it involves a deep alignment with what a church is all about. And churches can be quite different from one another. Before committing to anything, it's critical to investigate the situation adequately to discern whether the church is the right place for you to be.

This chapter will take you through important inquiries to make during your interview or orientation. These will help you gauge whether the church's culture, mission, and expectations are congruent with your calling and values and whether it's a place where you could really grow and contribute.

GRASPING THE CHURCH'S VISION AND MISSION

You should begin your interview by asking the church's leaders about its vision and mission. You are in a job where you need to know the "why" of everything the church does, and especially the "why" of the stuff that pertains to you and your work. Knowing the church's vision and mission is absolutely essential for conversations with church leaders.

1. *What is the church's vision or mission statement?* Every church should have a clear mission statement that defines its purpose and goals. Ask for this directly, and make sure it's something you connect with on a personal level. If you don't resonate with the church's mission, it will be difficult to feel fulfilled in your role.

2. *How is the church's mission being fulfilled in day-to-day operations?* It's one thing to have a mission statement on paper, but it's another to see that mission lived out practically. Ask how the church's vision influences its programming, decision-making, and community outreach. Look for specific examples of how the mission is being carried out in daily ministry.

EVALUATING THE CULTURE OF THE CHURCH

A church's culture shapes all aspects of its operation, from the manner in which the staff interacts with one another to the manner in which the church makes decisions. Working in a church with a culture opposite of your own can lead to conflict at best and premature departure at worst. For these reasons, assessing the church culture is an enormously important first step. Once you enter a church and begin to operate within its culture, it's much harder to leave.

1. *Describe the kind of culture the church staff has.* What is the staff's dynamic? How does the staff operate—collaboratively or as a top-down hierarchy? Is there a strong sense of community among the staff, or is more of it happening on an individual basis?

   Understanding the church staff's internal dynamics can give you a clearer picture of whether the culture suits your work style and your ministry personality.

2. *What are the church's core values?* In what ways do these values affect the church's approach to ministry and to the relationships between staff and congregants? Ensure that what the church staff values aligns with what you hold as your own topline priorities.

3. *How closely do the church staff and leadership follow the teachings and practices they preach?* Whether as a church or a staff, are they living out the doctrine and the ministry practices they espouse? Ask for some concrete, "real life" examples of this.

EXPECTATIONS FOR LIFESTYLE AND CONDUCT

You're seeking a church that's genuinely practicing its mission—one that's not just sending a message but is substantially connected to what it's doing in the community and beyond. You're also seeking a role where there's an alignment between your conduct and lifestyle choices and what the church expects of its staff.

1. *What does your church expect in terms of my lifestyle beyond the office?* Some congregations have remarkably detailed and even demanding requirements for their staff when it comes to personal living, daily habits, and social media. I consider it a must to know what the governing virtues, vices, and habits are

that I need to embody if I am going to serve that congregation. I also think it is wise and necessary to consider the alignment of those with my own set of virtues, vices, and habits.

2. *Are there any family or relational expectations that come with this position?* Does serving on the staff mean that all my family members must be members of that church? Must they be present at all services and events?

Unspoken expectations can often cause tension or confusion down the line. Be clear about whether staff members are expected to attend all church services or events, and whether family members are expected to be involved in the church as well.

LEADERSHIP STRUCTURE AND DECISION-MAKING

Understanding how leadership works at the church is critical, as this will influence how you interact with your supervisors and colleagues, as well as how decisions are made that affect your role.

1. *Is the church pastor-centric, elder-led, or staff-driven?* Different churches have different leadership models. Some churches are heavily pastor- centric, where the senior pastor makes most of the decisions. Others are led by a board of elders, deacons, or trustees. In staff-driven models, ministry leaders have more autonomy. Understanding where authority lies will help you navigate your role and relationships.

2. *How is conflict resolved among staff members and leadership?* Ask about how conflicts are handled. Churches, like any organization, will face disagreements or tension among staff. Understanding the processes in place for conflict resolution

will give you a sense of whether the church has healthy ways of addressing issues.

3. *Does the leadership encourage staff development and personal growth?* Ask whether the leadership invests in the personal and professional growth of staff members. Are there opportunities for continued education, mentorship, or leadership development? A healthy church culture encourages growth and learning among its staff.

CHURCH'S POLITICAL AND SOCIAL JUSTICE STANCES

In today's world, churches are often asked to take a stance on political or social justice issues. While this can be a sensitive topic, it's important to understand where the church stands on these issues and whether you are comfortable aligning with that stance.

1. *What is the church's position on political or social justice issues?* If the church takes a strong position on political matters or social justice causes, it's essential to know whether you're expected to represent those stances publicly as a staff member. Some churches may take a more neutral approach, while others are actively involved in advocacy or activism. Be clear about what role, if any, you're expected to play in these efforts.

ADDRESSING POTENTIAL CHALLENGES

No church is perfect, and it's important to go into a role with a clear understanding of any potential challenges or issues that might arise. Asking about the church's history and handling of difficult situations can give you insight into the culture and leadership.

1. *Has the church faced any scandals or major conflicts in recent years? How were they handled?* Every church goes through dif-

ficult seasons, and how they handle those challenges says a lot about the leadership and culture. Ask about any past scandals or conflicts, how they were resolved, and what steps were taken to ensure transparency and accountability.

2. *How does the church deal with mental health issues among staff members?* Ministry work can be emotionally and spiritually draining. Ask how the church supports staff members in dealing with stress, mental health, or burnout. Is there an open conversation about these issues, or are staff members expected to "tough it out" without support?

3. *Are there any expectations around handling failure or success within the role?* Understanding how the church celebrates successes and addresses failures is important for setting realistic expectations. Ask whether there's a culture of support and grace when mistakes happen, and how the leadership acknowledges successes within the staff.

REFLECTION QUESTIONS

1. How does the church's vision align with your personal calling and spiritual gifts?

2. What aspects of the church's culture and leadership structure are most important to you in a healthy work environment?

3. How can you ensure that you are stepping into a role where your personal values and lifestyle align with the church's expectations?

MENTOR MOMENTS FOR CHAPTER 3
QUESTIONS TO ASK BEFORE ACCEPTING A STAFF ROLE

Objective—Equip the new staff member with the knowledge and tools to ask insightful questions about their role, the church's culture, and expectations, ensuring they start with a clear understanding of their responsibilities and the church's vision.

Session Title—Asking the Right Questions: Building a Strong Foundation

Time Required—30–45 minutes

UNDERSTANDING THE CHURCH'S VISION AND MISSION

- **Mentor's Prompt**—"Knowing the church's vision and mission is essential for aligning your efforts with the church's goals. Let's discuss what you know about the church's mission and any questions you have about how your role supports that mission."

- **Questions for Reflection**

  ° What aspects of the church's vision resonate with you personally?

  ° Do you have any questions about how your role contributes to this mission?

NOTES

NAVIGATING CULTURE AND EXPECTATIONS

- **Mentor's Insight**—"Each church has its own unique culture and set of expectations for staff. It's important to understand these to ensure you're comfortable and prepared. I'll share some insights, and let's discuss any questions you have about how things work here."

- **Questions to Consider**

  ° Are there any questions you have about the day-to-day culture or expectations for staff?

  ° Is there anything you'd like to understand better about how our church approaches work-life balance, team dynamics, or communication?

NOTES

CLARIFYING YOUR ROLE AND RESPONSIBILITIES

- **Mentor's Guidance**—"Being clear on your responsibilities will help you start with confidence. Let's walk through your specific duties and talk about any additional areas you'd like to clarify."

- **Discussion Points**

  ° Do you feel clear on the primary tasks and responsibilities of your role?

  ° Is there anything you're unsure of regarding who you report to, team meetings, or goals for your position?

NOTES

FINAL REFLECTION AND PRAYER

- **Mentor's Closing Thought**—"Remember, asking questions is a sign of commitment and eagerness to integrate well. Take time to reflect on what you've learned, and don't hesitate to ask questions as you settle into your role."

- **Closing Prayer**—"Lord, thank You for bringing [staff member's name] to this ministry. Grant them clarity, understanding, and wisdom as they ask questions and learn about their new role. May they feel welcome and equipped to contribute to our church's vision. In Jesus' name, Amen."

CHAPTER 4

PEOPLE WHO WILL NOT DO WELL ON CHURCH STAFF

Working on church staff is a unique calling that requires dedication, integrity, and humility. However, certain personality traits and behaviors can be especially disruptive in ministry settings. This chapter focuses on four types of individuals who often struggle in church staff roles: The Lazy Person, the Gossip, the Manipulator, and the Opportunist. Each of these tendencies can be problematic, affecting not only the team dynamic but also the church's ability to serve its congregation and community effectively.

If you see any of these traits in yourself, use this chapter as a prompt for reflection and growth. If you find yourself working with colleagues who display these traits, the latter half of the chapter will offer practical tips on navigating those relationships.

THE LAZY PERSON

The Lazy Person struggles with motivation and avoids responsibilities, preferring to do the minimum required. While everyone occasionally feels unmotivated, chronic laziness on church staff creates a burden for other team members, who may need to pick up the slack.

Common Characteristics

- Avoidance of responsibility: Consistently shirks duties or redirects tasks to others.
- Procrastination: Delays tasks, often pushing deadlines or ignoring them entirely.
- Minimal initiative: Rarely contributes ideas or takes action unless explicitly asked.

Impact on Ministry

- Adds strain on other team members who feel obligated to cover their responsibilities.
- Limits the church's potential by reducing productivity and delaying projects.
- Creates resentment among the team, who may feel the lazy person is not pulling their weight.

Self-Reflection Encouragement

Consider Colossians 3:23, which reminds us to "work heartily, as for the Lord" (ESV). A heart for ministry requires a strong work ethic. If you find yourself frequently avoiding responsibility, ask God for motivation and consider seeking accountability with a mentor.

THE GOSSIP

Gossip can damage the foundation of trust within a team and create a toxic environment. The Gossip frequently shares private information, spreads rumors, or discusses sensitive topics without discretion, often causing division and discomfort among staff.

Common Characteristics

- Shares confidential information: Talks about sensitive or private matters, often under the guise of concern.
- Fosters division: Tends to form cliques or align with certain individuals, creating an "us versus them" dynamic.
- Focuses on negativity: Dwells on other people's struggles or faults instead of offering support.

Impact on Ministry

- Undermines trust, making it difficult for team members to collaborate openly.
- Discourages a spirit of unity, as people may avoid open communication for fear of being gossiped about.
- Damages the church's image, as congregants can sense when staff is divided.

Self-Reflection Encouragement

James 1:26 teaches, "If anyone thinks he is religious and does not bridle his tongue...this person's religion is worthless" (ESV). Reflect on how you use your words. Instead of focusing on others' shortcomings, commit to encouraging and supporting your team.

THE MANIPULATOR

The Manipulator uses their role to influence others for personal benefit, sometimes using their position or relationships to get what they want. Manipulators may appear helpful, but their actions often serve hidden agendas rather than the church's mission.

Common Characteristics

- Uses influence for self-interest: Makes decisions that benefit themselves rather than the church or team.
- Exploits relationships: Builds connections primarily to control or gain favor with others.
- Lacks transparency: Operates with hidden motives, causing mistrust and confusion among the team.

Impact on Ministry

- Reduces team morale, as others sense manipulation and lose trust.
- Diverts focus from the church's mission to individual agendas.
- Creates an environment of suspicion, which disrupts team cohesion.

Self-Reflection Encouragement

Jesus emphasized service, saying, "whoever would be great among you must be your servant" (Matthew 20:26, ESV). Church work is not about wielding influence for personal gain; it's about humility. If you find yourself motivated by self-interest, ask God for a heart that values service above recognition.

THE OPPORTUNIST

The Opportunist is driven by personal ambition and often seeks recognition or advancement at the expense of the team. While ambition can be healthy, the Opportunist is willing to prioritize personal success over the church's mission.

Common Characteristics

- Seeks the spotlight: Consistently desires attention or recognition for contributions.
- Pursues self-advancement: Treats the church role as a steppingstone for personal career growth.
- Undermines team goals: Focuses more on individual achievements than collective success.

Impact on Ministry

- Creates a competitive atmosphere that distracts from collaborative efforts.
- Frustrates other team members who feel overlooked or undervalued.
- Misaligns the church's purpose, as the focus shifts from God's mission to personal achievement.

Self-Reflection Encouragement

Philippians 2:3 encourages us, "Do nothing from selfish ambition...but in humility count others more significant than yourselves" (ESV). Reflect on whether you're prioritizing personal gains over the team's mission and consider how you can support others' success as much as your own.

WHAT TO DO IF YOUR COLLEAGUES EXHIBIT THESE TRAITS

When working with people who exhibit these traits, it's important to approach the situation with grace, patience, and discernment. Navigating these behaviors can be challenging, but a mindful approach can help maintain a positive and productive work environment.

If the Person Is a Coworker

Working alongside someone who exhibits these behaviors can be frustrating, but there are ways to handle the situation constructively.

1. *Set Personal Boundaries.* If you're working with someone prone to gossip or manipulation, set healthy boundaries to protect your focus and peace. Politely excuse yourself from conversations that turn negative and avoid sharing personal information that could be used against you.

2. *Model Positive Behavior.* Lead by example by demonstrating integrity, responsibility, and a team-first attitude. Often, people will follow the lead of those around them, especially when they see positive behaviors consistently modeled.

3. *Pray for Patience and Understanding.* Difficult relationships often improve when approached with patience and prayer. Ask God to give you a spirit of understanding and pray for your colleague to grow in areas where they may struggle.

If the Person Is Someone You Supervise

If you supervise someone who exhibits these behaviors, it's essential to address them constructively and with a focus on growth. Setting clear expectations and providing feedback can help the person develop healthier habits.

1. *Address the Behavior Directly but Compassionately.* Bring the issue up privately, focusing on specific behaviors and how they affect the team. Offer examples and explain why certain actions are disruptive, using a tone that is both firm and understanding.

2. *Encourage Accountability and Growth.* Provide resources for personal development, such as training, mentorship, or relevant readings. Encourage the person to seek accountability and remind them that growth in these areas will benefit both them and the ministry.

3. *Set Clear Expectations and Follow-Up.* After addressing the issue, establish clear expectations moving forward. Let the person know you're there to support their growth but hold them accountable to positive changes. Regular follow-ups can help them stay on track and give you a chance to offer guidance as needed.

REFLECTION QUESTIONS

1. Which of these traits resonates with you, and what steps can you take to ensure it doesn't affect your ministry?

2. If you work with someone who exhibits one of these tendencies, how can you set boundaries while maintaining a positive attitude?

3. How can prayer and patience help you approach difficult relationships within the church staff?

MENTOR MOMENTS FOR CHAPTER 4
PEOPLE WHO WILL NOT DO
WELL ON CHURCH STAFF

Objective—Encourage the new staff member to reflect on the types of attitudes and behaviors that can hinder ministry, promoting self-awareness and emphasizing the importance of integrity, humility, and teamwork in church staff roles.

Session Title—Thriving in Ministry: Embracing Positive Traits and Avoiding Pitfalls

Time Required—30–45 minutes

REFLECTING ON INTEGRITY AND HUMILITY

- **Mentor's Prompt**—"Working on church staff requires a heart for service, integrity, and humility. Let's discuss the types of behaviors that can challenge a healthy ministry environment and ways to make sure we are each serving with a pure heart."
- **Questions to Consider**
  ° How do you think integrity and humility contribute to a strong, effective church team?
  ° What steps can you take to remain self-aware and open to growth?

NOTES

RECOGNIZING UNHELPFUL TRAITS AND ENCOURAGING ACCOUNTABILITY

- **Mentor's Insight**—"Being aware of unhelpful traits, like gossip, laziness, or manipulation, can help us guard against them in ourselves and others. Let's go over how accountability within the team helps us uphold a positive culture."
- **Questions for Reflection**
  - How do you respond to feedback, especially if it's challenging?
  - Is there someone you trust who can hold you accountable as you grow in this role?

NOTES

STRIVING TO SUPPORT AND BUILD UP THE TEAM

- **Mentor's Guidance**—"Every member of the church staff contributes to the overall health of the team. Let's discuss ways you can actively work to build up and support your team, as well as keep your focus on serving others."
- **Discussion Points**
  - What are some actions or attitudes you can adopt to strengthen team unity?
  - How can you encourage your teammates in their own roles?

NOTES

FINAL REFLECTION AND PRAYER

- **Mentor's Closing Thought**—"Ministry is a team effort, and each of us has an important role. Take time to reflect on the qualities that contribute to healthy teamwork and pray for strength and grace to maintain a positive, supportive attitude."

- **Closing Prayer**—"Lord, thank You for this team and the calling You've placed on each of us. Help [staff member's name] to serve with integrity, humility, and a spirit that encourages others. May their actions build up the team and bring honor to You. In Jesus' name, Amen."

CHAPTER 5

REPRESENTING THE CHURCH IN PUBLIC LIFE

As a member of church staff, you represent more than just yourself—you are a reflection of your church and an ambassador for the kingdom of God. This responsibility impacts how you live your life, how you interact with others, and even what you post on social media. Your actions, both in public and private, can influence how others perceive your church and God's work within it. While this role may come with a level of scrutiny that can feel unfair, it's an opportunity to witness to others, reflecting God's love, truth, and grace in everyday interactions.

This chapter explores the importance of maintaining a positive reputation, balancing personal identity with church representation, and practical ways to honor this calling with integrity.

WHY OUTSIDE REPUTATION MATTERS

Maintaining a positive reputation is crucial in ministry, and the Bible speaks clearly about this. In Proverbs 22:1, we're reminded,

"A good name is more desirable than great riches; to be esteemed is better than silver or gold." Your reputation as a church staff member reflects not only on you but also on the church and God's kingdom. When people see you living with integrity and compassion, it strengthens trust and invites others into a relationship with God.

1. *Reflecting God's Character.* As representatives of Christ, we are called to live out our faith daily, showing kindness, humility, and patience. Paul emphasized this in 2 Corinthians 5:20: "We are therefore Christ's ambassadors, as though God were making his appeal through us." When your actions reflect these qualities, you allow others to see God's character in you.

2. *Building Trust in the Community.* A church's reputation in its community plays a vital role in its ability to minister effectively. First Thessalonians 5:22 advises us to "abstain from all appearance of evil" (KJV). This means avoiding actions or situations that could be misinterpreted or cause others to stumble. By being mindful of your words and actions, you foster trust and demonstrate respect for those watching.

Over my years in ministry, I've had countless people approach me to show videos or social media posts of church staff doing things they found provocative. If I had a dollar for every time this happened, I'd be rich. I'm not saying don't have fun—please, enjoy life! But recognize that being on church staff comes with a level of scrutiny that, while sometimes unfair, is understandable when you're leading people who are looking to you as an example.

PRACTICAL WAYS TO REPRESENT THE CHURCH WELL

1. *Consistency Between Private and Public Life.* Living with integrity means your values and actions are the same, regardless

of whether you're at work or in a personal setting. Jesus spoke about the importance of authenticity in Matthew 5:16: "Let your light shine before others, that they may see your good deeds and glorify your Father in heaven." Consistency in your actions creates trust, showing others that your faith is genuine.

2. *Mindfulness on Social Media.* Social media is a powerful tool, but it also requires careful thought. As you post, remember that your words and images are visible to a wide audience, and they reflect your values. Colossians 4:5–6 encourages us to be wise in how we act toward others, with our speech always being gracious and seasoned with salt. Avoid content that could be divisive or provoke unnecessary controversy and think about how each post might influence others' perception of your faith and your church.

3. *Community Engagement and Presence.* Actively participating in community events and building connections outside of church creates goodwill and trust. James 1:27 reminds us that true religion is shown through caring for others and living without hypocrisy. When you are visible in the community, you become a bridge for people to connect with the church, showing God's love in practical ways.

4. *Graceful Conflict Resolution.* How you handle conflict reflects on the church and the kingdom of God. Proverbs 15:1 says, "A gentle answer turns away wrath, but a harsh word stirs up anger." When disagreements arise, approach them with humility and grace, seeking peaceful resolutions. The way you handle conflict can be a powerful witness, showing others that the church values reconciliation and unity.

BALANCING PERSONAL IDENTITY WITH CHURCH REPRESENTATION

While you represent the church, it's also important to stay true to yourself. Balancing your personal identity with the responsibility of church representation allows you to serve authentically, showing others that faith isn't about perfection but about sincerity and growth.

1. *Staying Authentic.* Authenticity builds trust and makes you more approachable. People are drawn to staff members who are genuine and relatable, not those who seem untouchable or overly polished. In 1 Peter 5:5, we are encouraged to "clothe yourselves with humility." Being open about your own journey allows others to see you as a real person, which fosters meaningful connections.

2. *Setting Personal Boundaries.* While being transparent, it's also important to set boundaries around what you share publicly versus what remains private. This is essential for protecting your own well-being and ensuring that personal thoughts don't become confused with church positions.

Boundaries help you navigate when to speak for the church and when to share personal insights, preserving your own mental and emotional health.

3. *Representing the Church Without Losing Individuality.* Your unique gifts, personality, and experiences are an asset to your ministry. As long as they align with the church's values, embracing who you are can make you a more effective witness. Romans 12:4–6 reminds us that we all have different gifts and roles within the body of Christ and using those in service to the church honors God's design.

MAINTAINING A POSITIVE ONLINE PRESENCE

Social media can serve as a platform for positive influence, but it can also harm reputations when used carelessly. Consider the following tips for ensuring your online presence aligns with your role as a church staff member.

1. *Be Intentional.* Avoid posting impulsively, especially when feeling strong emotions. Take time to reflect on whether your words or images will build others up or risk causing misunderstandings.

2. *Share Positivity.* Focus on content that uplifts, encourages, and aligns with your church's values. This doesn't mean you can't share personal interests but be mindful of how each post represents your faith and your role.

3. *Respect Confidentiality.* As a church staff member, you may have access to sensitive information. Ensure you maintain confidentiality and don't share anything online that could compromise your role, or the trust people place in you.

THE PRIVILEGE AND RESPONSIBILITY OF REPRESENTATION

Representing the church and God's kingdom is both a privilege and a responsibility. It's an opportunity to make a positive impact, to show others the love and grace of God, and to build trust with those who may be exploring faith. This role requires mindfulness, integrity, and humility, but it's also incredibly rewarding. When you carry out this responsibility well, you create a space where others feel welcome, safe, and valued.

I have seen how simple acts of kindness, authentic relationships, and consistent integrity can make an enormous difference. People remember how you make them feel more than what you say or do. If you consistently demonstrate love, respect, and grace, you're creating an open door for others to experience God through you.

REFLECTION QUESTIONS

1. How can you ensure that your actions, both privately and publicly, reflect the values of your church and your faith?

2. In what ways can you use social media as a positive tool for representing your church and God's kingdom?

3. What steps can you take to balance your personal identity with the responsibility of representing the church authentically?

MENTOR MOMENTS FOR CHAPTER 5
REPRESENTING THE CHURCH IN PUBLIC LIFE

Objective—Help the new staff member understand the responsibility of representing both the church and God's kingdom with integrity, encouraging them to be mindful of their actions and words, both in and outside of church settings.

Session Title—Being an Ambassador: Representing the Church and Christ

Time Required—30–45 minutes

UNDERSTANDING THE RESPONSIBILITY OF REPRESENTATION

- **Mentor's Prompt**—"Working in church ministry means representing both our local church and the kingdom of God. Let's reflect on what it means to be an ambassador for Christ in everything you do, from your interactions to your online presence."

- **Questions to Consider**
  - What are some ways you can actively reflect God's love and grace in your role?
  - How do you think your actions, both at work and outside of it, influence others' views of the church?

MAINTAINING CONSISTENCY BETWEEN PRIVATE AND PUBLIC LIFE

- **Mentor's Insight**—"As an ambassador for Christ, consistency is key. Let's talk about why it's important to live with integrity, showing the same values in private as you do publicly."

- **Questions for Reflection**
  - ° How do you ensure that your private life aligns with the values you represent as a church staff member?
  - ° Are there areas where you feel you need more support to maintain this consistency?

NOTES

NAVIGATING SOCIAL MEDIA AND PUBLIC INTERACTIONS WITH WISDOM

- **Mentor's Guidance**—"Social media and public interactions can be challenging to navigate. Let's discuss how you can use these platforms responsibly to represent the church positively, while being mindful of personal boundaries."
- **Discussion Points**
  - ° How can you use social media to reflect your faith and the church's values?
  - ° Are there any personal guidelines you'd like to set to ensure your online presence aligns with your role?

NOTES

FINAL REFLECTION AND PRAYER

- **Mentor's Closing Thought**—"Representing Christ and the church is an honor and a responsibility. Take some time to pray for guidance as you serve as an ambassador, asking God to help you live a life that reflects His love and truth."

- **Closing Prayer**—"Lord, thank You for the privilege of representing Your kingdom. Help [staff member's name] to honor You in their actions, words, and presence. Give them wisdom and strength to reflect Your love to others, bringing glory to Your name. In Jesus' name, Amen."

CHAPTER 6

WORSHIPING WHERE YOU WORK

One of the most challenging aspects of church staff life is the overlap between your spiritual journey and your professional responsibilities. When your workplace is also your place of worship, it's easy to find yourself so immersed in the duties of ministry that you lose the personal connection with God that brought you to ministry in the first place. This chapter is about maintaining your spiritual vitality and ensuring that you continue to worship, even when worship becomes a part of your job.

In the early days of my ministry leadership, I began to notice something troubling among my staff members. During a team meeting, I decided to ask each person a series of questions about their spiritual life: When was the last time you prayed outside of church meetings? When did you last read your Bible for personal growth, or shared your faith with someone who wasn't already in church? To my surprise, most of my staff couldn't remember. They hadn't been spending personal time with God in weeks or even months. Their roles had become primarily professional, and their spiritual lives were dwindling.

I don't share this to condemn anyone—it's a common issue church staff encounters. We're human, and the lines between personal worship and professional responsibilities can blur. But if you're not careful, you can end up merely fulfilling the tasks of ministry without nurturing the relationship with God that makes it all meaningful. This chapter encourages you to set aside the time, space, and intentionality needed to keep your faith alive and vibrant.

KEEPING YOUR RELATIONSHIP WITH GOD CENTRAL

One of the biggest pitfalls of working in ministry is mistaking work for worship. There's a distinct difference between preparing a sermon, running a program, or counseling a congregant and spending time with God for your own growth. While God can certainly speak to you through the work you do, that's not a substitute for personal worship, prayer, and time in His Word.

To maintain your relationship with God, carve out time that is just for you and Him. Early mornings, quiet evenings, or lunch breaks can become sacred moments. "But when you pray, go into your room, close the door and pray to your Father, who is unseen" (Matthew 6:6).

These words remind us that true worship is often private, away from the demands of work and public ministry.

Ways to Cultivate Personal Worship

1. *Daily Devotion.* Set aside time every day, even if it's only ten or fifteen minutes, to read the Bible, pray, or reflect quietly. Whether you prefer structured devotionals or simply reading

through a book of the Bible, let this time be just between you and God.

2. *Sabbath Rest.* Taking a true Sabbath can be challenging when you're involved in Sunday services but find a day or even an afternoon to rest and refresh spiritually. Spend time in nature, read, pray, and let God renew you.

3. *Worship Beyond Work.* Attend worship services without responsibilities whenever you can. Find a place where you can worship without worrying about logistics or attend events at another church. This will allow you to be fully present in worship as a participant, rather than as a staff member.

MAINTAINING PERSPECTIVE AS BOTH WORSHIPER AND WORKER

Working on church staff requires you to be both a worshiper and a worker, and navigating these roles can be tricky. It's essential to keep perspective, recognizing that while you serve others, you also need spiritual feeding and growth. In the book of Luke, Jesus told Martha, "Martha, Martha, you are anxious and troubled about many things, but one thing is necessary. Mary has chosen the good portion, which will not be taken away from her" (Luke 10:41–42, ESV).

Jesus' reminder to Martha encourages us to prioritize being with God over merely working for Him.

This balance requires intentional boundaries. You may need to clarify your availability, explaining that certain times are set aside for personal growth. Make it clear to others—and to yourself—that worship is essential to your well-being as a ministry leader.

AVOIDING BURNOUT BY STAYING CONNECTED TO GOD

The weight of ministry can lead to burnout, especially if you neglect your personal relationship with God. Staying connected with Him is the best way to find strength, wisdom, and resilience. In Matthew 11:28, Jesus invites us, saying, "Come to me, all you who are weary and burdened, and I will give you rest." He assures us that His yoke is easy, and His burden is light (11:30).

Burnout often creeps in when the demands of work become too heavy, and we attempt to carry them alone. Take time to rest in God's presence, remembering that ministry is His work, not solely ours. Leaning into this truth can ease the burden and allow you to approach your role with joy and sustainability.

By staying connected to God through personal worship, you'll not only protect yourself from burnout but also find the strength to serve with genuine joy and purpose. This chapter is a reminder that you are part of the supporting cast in God's story—serving, but also deeply loved and cared for by Him.

REFLECTION QUESTIONS

1. How often do you spend time with God outside of work-related tasks?

2. What steps can you take to prioritize personal worship and devotion, even amid ministry demands?

3. How does your role as both worshiper and worker shape your view of your relationship with God?

MENTOR MOMENTS FOR CHAPTER 6
WORSHIPING WHERE YOU WORK

Objective—Help the new staff member understand the importance of maintaining a personal worship life outside of their job duties, ensuring they nurture their spiritual health and connection to God.

Session Title—Keeping Worship Alive: Maintaining Personal Faith in a Ministry Role

Time Required—30–45 minutes

RECOGNIZING THE DIFFERENCE BETWEEN WORK AND WORSHIP

- **Mentor's Prompt**—"Working in church ministry means it's easy to blur the line between worship and work. It's essential to maintain a personal relationship with God, separate from the responsibilities of your role. Let's talk about how you can keep your worship alive and meaningful."

- **Questions to Consider**

  ° How can you ensure you're spending personal time with God, apart from your job responsibilities?

  ° Are there any spiritual practices that help you connect deeply with God outside of work?

NOTES

DEVELOPING PERSONAL WORSHIP PRACTICES

- **Mentor's Insight**—"Setting aside regular time for personal worship is key to avoiding burnout and staying spiritually grounded. Let's discuss ways you can establish consistent practices, even when work gets busy."

- **Questions for Reflection**

  ° What time of day or week can you dedicate to personal worship, prayer, and study?

  ° Are there particular practices, like journaling, Scripture reading, or worship music, that help you connect with God?

NOTES

CREATING BOUNDARIES TO PROTECT YOUR WORSHIP TIME

- **Mentor's Guidance**—"It's essential to protect your personal worship time, even when ministry demands increase. Let's talk about boundaries that can help you keep your worship and relationship with God a priority."

- **Discussion Points**

  ° What boundaries can you set to ensure work doesn't take over your personal worship time?

  ° How will you communicate these boundaries, if needed, with colleagues or family?

NOTES

FINAL REFLECTION AND PRAYER

- **Mentor's Closing Thought**—"Your relationship with God is the foundation of your ministry. Take time to pray that He helps you maintain a strong, vibrant connection with Him, both inside and outside of work."

- **Closing Prayer**—"Lord, thank You for calling [staff member's name] to serve. Help them to seek You above all, protecting their worship and relationship with You. May their work flow out of their love for You, and may they be renewed in Your presence each day. In Jesus' name, Amen."

CHAPTER 7

EMOTIONAL AND SPIRITUAL WELL-BEING IN MINISTRY

Ministry is a calling that requires heart, dedication, and resilience. The emotional and spiritual demands of working in church staff roles can be incredibly fulfilling but also challenging, as you carry the weight of others' burdens while nurturing a congregation. This chapter explores practical ways to cultivate sustainable well-being by understanding your emotional, physical, spiritual, and relational health—grounded in Gallup's research on well-being.

Gallup has identified five critical areas of well-being that apply across careers, including ministry: Career Well-Being, Social Well-Being, Financial Well-Being, Physical Well-Being, and Community Well-Being. Maintaining balance in each of these areas helps create a foundation for thriving in ministry. Let's dive into each area and explore how it relates to church staff roles, with practical advice on building habits that protect your well-being.

RECOGNIZING THE SIGNS OF BURNOUT AND PRIORITIZING CAREER WELL-BEING

Career well-being centers on finding purpose and meaning in your work. In ministry, this sense of purpose often comes naturally, but the pressure to meet endless needs can strain your emotional and spiritual health, leading to burnout.

Common Signs of Burnout

1. *Emotional Exhaustion.* Feeling constantly drained can indicate burnout, as ministry demands often require deep emotional investment.

2. *Loss of Motivation.* Losing enthusiasm for your role can mean that your sense of purpose is being overshadowed by exhaustion.

3. *Increased Irritability.* Ministry burnout can lead to frustration or irritability toward others, making it harder to serve with grace.

4. *Difficulty Sleeping or Concentrating.* Mental fatigue often accompanies burnout, impacting sleep quality and focus.

Career Well-Being Tip: Avoid burnout by aligning your daily work with the church's mission and remembering your core reasons for serving. Reflect on your purpose, create realistic work boundaries, and don't hesitate to ask for support when you need it.

INVESTING IN SOCIAL WELL-BEING

Social connections are vital in ministry, as healthy relationships provide support and accountability. However, church staff roles can sometimes feel isolating due to the need for confidentiality or the weight of leadership responsibilities. Building authentic connections with both staff and peers outside of your ministry is essential for maintaining resilience.

1. *Find a Trusted Support System.* Surround yourself with a few trusted people who understand the unique challenges of ministry. This could be a small group, mentor, or fellow church leaders.

2. *Build Boundaries With Congregants.* While connections with congregants are important, it's crucial to have friendships where you can be fully transparent without the pressures of leadership.

Social Well-Being Tip: Encourage positive relationships both inside and outside of church work. Prioritizing social well-being will help you stay grounded, increase your resilience, and provide a support network for when ministry gets challenging.

PRACTICING FINANCIAL WELL-BEING

Financial well-being is about managing your resources in a way that minimizes stress. While few people enter ministry to become wealthy, financial pressures can affect even the most dedicated church staff members. A balanced approach to finances can reduce anxiety and help you serve without the burden of financial worry.

1. *Budget Wisely.* Ensure that your financial goals align with your ministry lifestyle. Stick to a budget that accommodates your needs, so you're not constantly worried about finances.

2. *Seek Guidance if Needed.* Financial counseling can be incredibly helpful, especially when balancing ministry salaries with the cost of living.

Financial Well-Being Tip: Create a financial plan that supports both your ministry work and personal needs, allowing you to serve with greater focus and peace.

MAINTAINING PHYSICAL WELL-BEING

Physical well-being is about staying active and taking care of your body to prevent fatigue and burnout. Ministry often requires high emotional and mental energy, and without physical self- care, it's easy to become depleted.

Personally, I find exercise—whether it's walking, jogging, or another form of physical activity—vital for stress management. Physical activities like painting and exercising are wonderful outlets that help me feel renewed and prepared to tackle ministry's unique challenges.

Physical Well-Being Practices

1. *Exercise Regularly.* Engage in physical activity that you enjoy, such as walking, jogging, or yoga. Physical exercise releases endorphins, helping you manage stress and stay focused.

2. *Prioritize Sleep.* Good rest is foundational to health. Make sleep a non-negotiable part of your self-care, setting regular bedtime routines to ensure you're fully rested.

3. *Take Breaks for Mental Rejuvenation.* Periodically taking a walk, painting, or just stepping away from your work helps maintain focus and increases resilience.

Physical Well-Being Tip: Regular exercise, sleep, and periodic breaks are essential to sustaining energy for long-term ministry. Prioritizing physical well-being helps you stay resilient and balanced.

CULTIVATING COMMUNITY WELL-BEING

Ministry work is deeply connected to the community, and healthy community well-being involves feeling connected and giving back meaningfully. Creating a sustainable approach to how you engage with your community will help you stay refreshed and avoid the trap of overworking.

1. *Set Realistic Goals for Community Engagement.* While it can be tempting to attend every event, prioritize those that align most closely with your role and capacity.

2. *Encourage Congregants to Serve.* Involve others in community work rather than taking on every responsibility yourself. By empowering others, you create a sustainable ministry environment and avoid taking on an unsustainable workload.

Community Well-Being Tip: Build community well-being by setting healthy boundaries and encouraging others to participate in community life. A sustainable approach helps you maintain energy and enthusiasm over the long term.

SUSTAINABLE SELF-CARE PRACTICES FOR MINISTRY

Sustainability in self-care means creating consistent, manageable habits that support well-being in all areas. For me, self-care includes painting, exercising, and writing, all of which give me an outlet for creativity, relaxation, and personal reflection. The key is to find practices that work for you and to make them a priority, especially when ministry demands increase.

1. *Integrate Creative Outlets.* Engaging in creative activities like painting or music can help reduce stress and foster mental clarity. Whether it's a hobby, artistic pursuit, or a quiet activi-

ty like reading, creative outlets help you decompress and gain new perspectives.

2. *Schedule Regular Breaks and Vacations.* Rest is essential. Taking time off—whether a weekly day of rest or a longer vacation—is crucial for maintaining well-being. There is no nobility in avoiding rest; without breaks, burnout becomes inevitable. Schedule these breaks in advance and protect them as essential for your health.

3. *Practice Saying No.* In ministry, it's easy to overcommit in the name of service. However, sustainable ministry requires knowing when to set boundaries. Be intentional about which tasks align with your purpose and avoid overextending yourself.

4. *Make Space for Spiritual Renewal.* Regular spiritual practices, like prayer and Bible reading, are essential for ministry. Set aside personal time for spiritual growth, separate from your work-related tasks. These moments of connection with God will help you stay spiritually strong, avoiding burnout and maintaining perspective.

REFLECTION QUESTIONS

1. Which of Gallup's areas of well-being do you find easiest to maintain, and which ones need more attention?

2. What activities or practices help you decompress and restore energy for ministry?

3. How can you make sustainable self-care a priority, ensuring you stay resilient in the long run?

MENTOR MOMENTS FOR CHAPTER 7
EMOTIONAL AND SPIRITUAL WELL-BEING IN MINISTRY

Objective—Help the new staff member recognize the importance of caring for their emotional and spiritual health, providing practical guidance on establishing habits and boundaries that promote resilience and prevent burnout.

Session Title—Nurturing Well-Being: Sustaining Health in Ministry

Time Required—30–45 minutes

UNDERSTANDING THE UNIQUE CHALLENGES OF MINISTRY

- **Mentor's Prompt**—"Working in ministry brings unique emotional and spiritual challenges that can take a toll if left unaddressed. Let's talk about some of these challenges and how you can prepare yourself to handle them."

- **Questions to Consider**

  ° What emotional or spiritual challenges do you anticipate in this role?

  ° How do you typically manage stress, and are there any new approaches you'd like to explore?

NOTES

BUILDING A ROUTINE FOR SELF-CARE AND SPIRITUAL RENEWAL

- **Mentor's Insight**—"Consistent self-care and spiritual practices are essential to thriving in ministry. Let's discuss practical ways you can maintain a healthy balance, ensuring you stay refreshed and connected to God."
- **Questions for Reflection**
  - ° What specific activities or practices renew your energy and keep you centered?
  - ° How can you incorporate these routines into your weekly schedule, even during busy seasons?

NOTES

SETTING BOUNDARIES TO PREVENT BURNOUT

- **Mentor's Guidance**—"Setting boundaries around work, personal time, and family is essential to prevent burnout. Let's talk about some boundaries you can establish to protect your well-being while serving in this role."
- **Discussion Points**
  - ° What boundaries will help you maintain a healthy balance between work and personal life?
  - ° Are there any areas where you foresee difficulty in setting boundaries, and how can we address those challenges?

NOTES

FINAL REFLECTION AND PRAYER

- **Mentor's Closing Thought**—"God desires you to be whole—emotionally, spiritually, and physically. Take time to reflect on how you can care for yourself so you can serve with joy, resilience, and strength."

- **Closing Prayer**—"Lord, thank You for the calling You have placed on [staff member's name]. Grant them wisdom and discipline to care for their emotional and spiritual health. Strengthen them for the work You have set before them and fill them with Your peace and joy each day. In Jesus' name, Amen."

CHAPTER 8

VOLUNTEERS—USING THE HELP AROUND YOU

Volunteers are the lifeblood of church ministry, the unsung heroes who offer their time, energy, and resources to support the church's mission. While church staff members carry out specific duties, it's the volunteers who bring extra hands and hearts to the work. They are often the first face visitors see and the ones who make events, services, and outreach initiatives possible. Working with volunteers effectively requires understanding their unique motivations, appreciating their contributions, and fostering an environment where they feel valued and equipped to serve.

I've had the privilege of working alongside countless volunteers. Some have been invaluable partners in ministry, while others have required more guidance and patience. Each person brings something unique, and as a staff member, your role is to nurture these relationships, keeping in mind that volunteers may not have the same experience or commitment level as staff. This chapter is dedicated to exploring the best ways to collaborate with volunteers, honor their contributions, and create a healthy, supportive environment for everyone involved.

UNDERSTANDING VOLUNTEER MOTIVATIONS

People volunteer in church for a variety of reasons. Some feel a spiritual calling to serve; others want to give back to a community that's been meaningful to them. Some volunteers join to build relationships, while others are passionate about a particular ministry, such as youth work, outreach, or music. Recognizing and understanding these motivations is key to working effectively with volunteers. When you understand why someone is serving, you can encourage them in ways that speak to their interests and passions, making them feel valued and appreciated.

Example: I once worked with a volunteer named Mark who faithfully assisted with our community outreach events. Mark wasn't looking for recognition; his motivation was deeply personal—he had been helped by a church during a difficult season in his own life and he wanted to give back. Knowing this allowed me to encourage Mark in a way that acknowledged his past experiences and kept him engaged, understanding that his work wasn't just about logistics; it was a form of gratitude and worship.

BUILDING RELATIONSHIPS WITH VOLUNTEERS

As a staff member, you have the unique responsibility of leading and supporting volunteers, often by cultivating relationships that are both professional and personal. Volunteers are giving their time freely, and while they may be committed, they aren't obligated to stay. Building strong, positive relationships with volunteers helps them feel connected to the ministry, valued as individuals, and more motivated to contribute.

1. *Get to Know Them Personally.* Taking time to learn about a volunteer's life outside of church helps create a bond that goes beyond tasks. Ask about their family, job, or interests. Show genuine interest in who they are and what they bring to the team. This small investment in relationship-building can make a huge difference in how connected and committed they feel.

2. *Appreciate Their Contributions Publicly and Privately.* Volunteers need to know their efforts are noticed and appreciated. Recognize their hard work in front of the congregation if appropriate but also make sure to thank them privately. A simple "thank you" can go a long way in building a culture of gratitude.

Some churches hold annual volunteer appreciation events, while others write personalized thank-you notes. Find what works best in your church context and commit to making volunteer appreciation a regular practice.

3. *Create Opportunities for Development and Growth.* Just because volunteers aren't paid doesn't mean they don't want to grow. Offer training, provide mentorship, and create opportunities for them to develop new skills. This investment shows you see their potential and you care about their personal development, not just their ability to complete a task. When volunteers feel they are growing, they are more likely to stay engaged and continue contributing.

WORKING WITH VOLUNTEERS EFFECTIVELY

Working with volunteers means balancing guidance with respect for their time and limitations. Unlike paid staff, volunteers may not be available 24/7 or able to handle every task perfectly. Knowing how to set expectations and communicate clearly can prevent misunderstandings and help you work together more effectively.

1. *Set Clear Expectations.* Being clear about what you need from a volunteer can prevent frustration on both sides. Communicate the purpose of the role, the time commitment involved, and any specific tasks or responsibilities. This helps volunteers understand what's expected of them and gives them the information they need to determine if they can commit fully.

2. *Provide Structure and Support.* Volunteers, especially new ones, may feel lost without guidance. Set them up for success by giving them a clear plan or schedule and being available to answer questions. A structured approach helps them feel confident in their roles and reassures them that their time is being used effectively.

3. *Encourage Feedback.* Volunteers often have valuable insights because they experience the church from both the inside and outside. Encourage them to share their thoughts on the ministry, the church's needs, or any challenges they face. Listening to their feedback not only helps improve the ministry but also shows them their voice matters.

4. *Respect Their Time and Boundaries.* Unlike staff, volunteers often have other major commitments, like full-time jobs or family responsibilities. Respect their time by keeping meetings efficient and only asking for their help within reasonable

limits. When you show respect for their boundaries, they're more likely to feel valued and willing to continue serving.

RECOGNIZING THE DUAL NATURE OF VOLUNTEERS: HELP OR HINDRANCE

Volunteers are wonderful assets, but not every volunteer is an immediate fit. Some may unintentionally create challenges due to lack of experience, conflicting personalities, or simply a misunderstanding of their role. Knowing how to navigate these situations with grace and honesty is essential for a healthy ministry environment.

I once worked with a volunteer who was extremely enthusiastic but struggled to follow directions. They had a heart for serving but often deviated from the plan, causing confusion for others. I realized they needed more structure and guidance, so I paired them with a more experienced volunteer who could provide mentorship. This adjustment helped them feel supported and gave them a framework to thrive within.

If a volunteer consistently disrupts the ministry or refuses to adapt to the team's needs, it may be necessary to have a candid conversation. Approach these conversations with grace, focusing on the overall goals of the ministry and offering suggestions for other areas where they might serve more effectively.

VOLUNTEERS AS PARTNERS IN MINISTRY

Volunteers are more than just extra hands—they're partners in the church's mission. When you view them as collaborators rather than helpers, you create a culture of respect and shared purpose. Volunteers bring fresh perspectives, valuable skills, and a willingness to serve that can inspire the entire church staff. By treating them as partners, you empower them to take ownership of the ministry and encourage a deeper level of engagement.

Building a thriving ministry with volunteers is about creating a team that feels united in purpose. When volunteers see their contributions as essential to the church's mission, they're more likely to stay committed, even through challenges. As a staff member, nurturing this sense of partnership and shared vision can strengthen the entire church community.

REFLECTION QUESTIONS

1. How can you better understand the motivations of the volunteers you work with, and how might this understanding improve your relationship with them?

2. In what ways can you honor and appreciate the contributions of volunteers both publicly and privately?

3. What steps can you take to ensure volunteers feel valued, equipped, and connected to the church's mission?

MENTOR MOMENTS FOR CHAPTER 8
VOLUNTEERS—USING THE HELP AROUND YOU

Objective—Help the new staff member understand the value of volunteers, providing guidance on how to build positive relationships, delegate effectively, and encourage a sense of teamwork and purpose among volunteers.

Session Title—Leading with Others: Engaging and Empowering Volunteers

Time Required—30–45 minutes

RECOGNIZING THE VALUE OF VOLUNTEERS

- **Mentor's Prompt**—"Volunteers are essential to the life of the church. Each one brings unique gifts and a willingness to serve. Let's talk about the importance of valuing volunteers and how you can show appreciation for their efforts."

- **Questions to Consider**

  ° How can you show volunteers that their contributions are valued and essential to the ministry?

  ° In what ways can you actively support and encourage them?

NOTES

DELEGATING EFFECTIVELY AND SETTING CLEAR EXPECTATIONS

- **Mentor's Insight**—"Delegation is key to successful teamwork, especially when working with volunteers who may have varying schedules and commitments. Let's discuss how you can delegate tasks effectively and communicate expectations clearly."

- **Questions for Reflection**
  - How comfortable are you with delegating tasks, and what areas might require more guidance?
  - What methods can you use to ensure volunteers understand their roles and responsibilities?

NOTES

BUILDING RELATIONSHIPS AND FOSTERING A TEAM ENVIRONMENT

- **Mentor's Guidance**—"Creating a positive and collaborative environment makes volunteers feel connected to the mission. Let's talk about how you can build relationships with volunteers and foster a team spirit that encourages unity and shared purpose."

- **Discussion Points**
  - What actions can you take to develop strong, respectful relationships with volunteers?
  - How can you cultivate a sense of teamwork and belonging within the volunteer group?

NOTES

FINAL REFLECTION AND PRAYER

- **Mentor's Closing Thought**—"Volunteers are a blessing to the church, and serving alongside them is a privilege. Take time to reflect on how you can be a source of encouragement and leadership for them as you work together for God's kingdom."

- **Closing Prayer**—"Lord, thank You for the volunteers who serve faithfully in this church. Help [staff member's name] to lead them with grace, wisdom, and appreciation. May they create an environment where every volunteer feels valued and encouraged to serve with joy. In Jesus' name, Amen."

CHAPTER 9

UNDERSTANDING CHURCH CULTURE AND LEADERSHIP STYLES

Each church has a unique culture that reflects its history, community, and leadership. Understanding this culture is crucial for anyone considering a church staff role, as it can shape everything from daily routines to decision-making processes. Church culture affects how people interact, resolve conflicts, and pursue the church's mission. By understanding a church's culture and leadership style, you can navigate your role with greater confidence and contribute effectively to the team.

In my experience, thriving while on church staff requires a willingness to adapt to the church's existing culture while also bringing your own strengths to the table. Every church has its own rhythm and expectations, and each leader has a unique approach to guiding the team. By recognizing and respecting these nuances, you'll be better equipped to integrate into the church and make a meaningful impact.

IDENTIFYING AND ADAPTING TO CHURCH CULTURE

A church's culture is often shaped by its history, values, and the personality of its leaders. Some churches prioritize tradition and structure, while others lean toward flexibility and creativity.

Some churches emphasize evangelism and outreach, while others focus on discipleship and spiritual formation. Understanding a church's culture involves observing its norms, asking questions, and listening to how people talk about the church's mission and goals.

I currently serve at a church where the culture is highly relationship-oriented. Meetings often begin with casual conversations, and decisions are made through consensus. In contrast, I had previously worked at a church with a very task-focused culture, where meetings were long and tense, and efficiency was highly valued. Adapting to this new relationship-oriented environment took time, but it helped me learn the value of building connections before diving into work. This adjustment made my work more effective and showed me how embracing a church's culture can lead to greater harmony and purpose.

When joining a new church staff, take time to observe the culture and ask questions to understand it fully. Who makes the decisions? How does the team communicate? How are conflicts resolved? Understanding these dynamics can help you adapt to the environment and approach your role in a way that resonates with the team.

NAVIGATING DIFFERENT LEADERSHIP STYLES

Leadership in a church can vary widely, and it's important to understand the style of the pastor or leader you'll be working under. Some churches are pastor-centric, where the senior pastor has a significant amount of influence and authority. Others are led by a board of elders, deacons, or trustees, where decisions are made collectively. Still others might have a staff-driven model, where various department heads or ministry leaders hold significant decision-making power. Knowing the church's leadership structure helps you understand who is responsible for what and how to align your efforts with their vision.

Common Leadership Styles in Churches

1. *Pastor-Centric Leadership.* In pastor-centric churches, the senior pastor often has the final say on most decisions and serves as the primary visionary for the church. This structure can be efficient, as decisions are made quickly, and the direction is clear. However, working in a pastor-centric church requires understanding and respecting the pastor's authority and vision. This style can be challenging if you're used to more collaborative decision-making. It's essential to have open communication with the pastor to ensure alignment with their vision and avoid misunderstandings.

2. *Elder or Trustee-Led Leadership.* Churches led by elders, deacons, or trustees often have a team-oriented approach to leadership. Decisions are made through discussions and votes, and authority is distributed among several leaders. This style can be beneficial for fostering diverse perspectives and ensuring that decisions reflect the church's overall values. However, it may also lead to slower decision-making processes, as consensus must be reached. In this setting, patience and flexibility are key, as decisions may take time and require input from multiple people.

3. *Staff-Driven Leadership.* In a staff-driven model, department heads or ministry leaders hold significant decision-making

power, and the church often values the contributions of each staff member. This environment can be empowering, as each person has a level of autonomy in their area. However, it also requires strong teamwork and communication to keep everyone aligned. In a staff-driven church, it's important to collaborate effectively with others, respecting each person's role and expertise while contributing your own insights and ideas.

4. *Collaborative Leadership.* Some churches take a collaborative approach, blending aspects of each model. For example, the pastor may provide overall vision, while elders and staff members contribute ideas and share responsibilities. In a collaborative church, everyone's input is valued, and there is a strong emphasis on teamwork. If you're working in a collaborative environment, actively participate in discussions and bring your unique perspective to the table. Being open to others' ideas and fostering unity helps create a healthy, dynamic team that can accomplish great things.

ASSESSING IF YOU FIT WITHIN THE CHURCH'S LEADERSHIP STRUCTURE

Working under different leadership styles requires adaptability and self-awareness. Reflect on your own leadership preferences and consider how they align with the church's approach.

Some people thrive in highly structured environments, while others prefer a more flexible, collaborative style. Understanding your own preferences can help you determine whether a church's leadership structure will be a good fit.

Ask yourself the following questions to gauge your fit:

- Are you comfortable with authority being centralized, or do you prefer shared decision making?
- Do you value efficiency and direct communication, or do you prefer a more relational approach?
- Are you open to adapting your style to meet the church's needs, even if it differs from what you're used to?
- These questions can provide clarity and help you navigate the dynamics of church leadership with a healthy perspective.

ALIGNING YOUR ROLE WITH THE CHURCH'S CULTURE AND LEADERSHIP

Once you understand the church's culture and leadership style, consider how you can best align your work with these dynamics. If the church values tradition, focus on ways to honor that tradition while bringing fresh ideas. If it's a church that prioritizes outreach, look for opportunities to contribute to its mission of reaching the community. Adapting your approach to align with the church's values demonstrates respect for the culture and helps you integrate more smoothly into the team.

I once coached a children's ministry director named Rachel who joined a church with a highly outreach-oriented culture. She had previously worked in a smaller, discipleship-focused church and was used to creating in-depth lesson plans for smaller groups. To align with the new church's outreach goals, she adapted her approach to design children's programs that attracted families from the community. By embracing the church's culture, she helped expand the children's ministry in a way that resonated with the church's vision.

Aligning your role with the church's culture is about finding a balance between bringing your strengths and adapting to the church's needs. When you make this adjustment, your work feels more purposeful, and you become a valuable contributor to the church's mission.

REFLECTION QUESTIONS

How would you describe the culture of your church or the church you're considering, and how does it align with your own values?

Which leadership style resonates most with you, and how can you adapt if the church's style is different?

What are practical ways you can align your work with the church's mission and cultural values?

MENTOR MOMENTS FOR CHAPTER 9 UNDERSTANDING CHURCH CULTURE AND LEADERSHIP STYLES

Objective—Help the new staff member gain insight into the church's unique culture and leadership style, equipping them to adapt and work effectively within the existing structure.

Session Title—Embracing the Culture: Navigating Church Dynamics and Leadership Styles

Time Required—30–45 minutes

LEARNING THE CHURCH'S CULTURE AND VALUES

- Mentor's Prompt—"Every church has its own culture, shaped by its history, values, and people. Understanding this culture helps you align with the church's mission and engage well with the congregation. Let's discuss what you've observed about our culture and any questions you may have."

- Questions to Consider

  ° What elements of the church's culture stand out to you so far?

  ° How do you see yourself fitting into this culture, and are there areas where you need more clarity?

NOTES

ADAPTING TO DIFFERENT LEADERSHIP STYLES

- **Mentor's Insight**—"Church leadership styles can vary significantly. Some churches are more pastor-led, while others may rely on a team of deacons, elders, or staff. Let's discuss how you can work effectively within our church's structure and adapt to leadership styles you encounter."

- **Questions for Reflection**

  ° How would you describe your own leadership style, and how do you think it aligns with our church's approach?

  ° Are there any challenges you anticipate with different leadership styles, and how can we address those?

NOTES

NAVIGATING RELATIONSHIPS WITH CHURCH LEADERS AND CONGREGANTS

- **Mentor's Guidance**—"Building positive relationships with church leaders and congregants is essential to your role. Let's talk about how to approach these relationships with respect and understanding, and how to handle potential disagreements gracefully."

- **Discussion Points**

  ° How can you show respect for church leadership while also offering your unique perspective?

  ° What steps will you take to foster trust and rapport with both leaders and congregants?

NOTES

FINAL REFLECTION AND PRAYER

- **Mentor's Closing Thought**—"Adapting to the church's culture and leadership style is a journey. Take time to reflect on how you can contribute to this community with humility and respect, embracing both the unique culture and the people you'll be serving alongside."

- **Closing Prayer**—"Lord, thank You for bringing [staff member's name] to this church family. Help them to understand and embrace the culture here, respecting those in leadership and serving with a humble heart. May their work honor You and strengthen the unity of our church. In Jesus' name, Amen."

CHAPTER 10

MY PASTOR IS MY BOSS!— NAVIGATING A DUAL RELATIONSHIP

One of the most unique and sometimes challenging dynamics in church staff life is working for a pastor who serves not only as your spiritual leader but also as your direct supervisor. This dual relationship can be a delicate balancing act—your pastor is the one you look to for spiritual guidance, but they are also responsible for evaluating your work performance, providing direction, and making leadership decisions that affect your daily responsibilities. Navigating this relationship with grace, respect, and understanding is essential to thriving as a church staff member.

In this chapter, we'll explore how to put into perspective the dual role of pastor and boss, how to nurture both sides of the relationship, and what to do when you disagree with the pastor's direction. We'll also draw lessons from the biblical story of David and Saul, offering practical insights on how to respect leadership even when challenges arise.

UNDERSTANDING THE DUAL ROLE

The dual role of pastor and boss can feel complex at times because it involves two distinct aspects of the relationship. On the one hand, you view your pastor as your spiritual guide, someone you respect for their wisdom, leadership, and care for your spiritual well-being. On the other hand, they are also your boss—the person responsible for ensuring you meet job expectations, manage your responsibilities, and align with the church's vision. Balancing these roles requires clarity and boundaries to avoid confusion and potential conflict.

The first step in navigating this dynamic is to recognize that these roles are distinct but not mutually exclusive. Your pastor may make decisions as a boss that don't necessarily align with your spiritual expectations, and that's okay. Understanding when they are speaking to you as a spiritual leader versus a supervisor can help you frame your responses and manage your expectations. Similarly, it's important to separate work performance feedback from spiritual direction.

NURTURING BOTH SIDES OF THE RELATIONSHIP

Building a healthy working relationship with your pastor requires intentionality. The key is to nurture both aspects of the relationship—respecting their authority as a boss while valuing their role as a spiritual leader.

1. *Communicate Clearly.* Clear communication is vital in maintaining a healthy relationship with your pastor. If you're unsure whether feedback or direction is coming from a spiritual place or a work-related one, don't be afraid to ask for clarification. Understanding the intent behind the feedback helps you avoid misunderstandings and keeps the relationship in balance.

Regular check-ins with your pastor about both your spiritual growth and work performance can create opportunities for open communication and mutual understanding.

2. *Respect the Leadership Structure.* Even when the lines between pastor and boss blur, it's important to respect the leadership structure in place. Acknowledge that your pastor has been entrusted with leading the church both spiritually and operationally, and that decisions they make are likely influenced by factors you may not always see. Your job as a staff member is to support the church's mission, even when you don't agree with every decision. By showing respect for the leadership structure, you demonstrate humility and a willingness to serve, which can strengthen your relationship with your pastor.

3. *Maintain Healthy Boundaries.* One of the challenges in a pastor-boss relationship is maintaining healthy boundaries between work life and spiritual life. It's easy for the two to blend together, but creating clear boundaries helps prevent burnout and emotional strain. For example, if your pastor offers spiritual counsel during a personal hardship, recognize that this conversation is separate from your work responsibilities. Setting these boundaries allows you to maintain a healthy work-life balance while also receiving the spiritual guidance you need.

WHAT TO DO WHEN YOU DISAGREE

Disagreements are inevitable in any working relationship, and church staff positions are no exception. Disagreeing with your pastor on the direction of the church or a particular decision can be challenging because of their dual role. It's important to approach disagreements with grace, humility, and a willingness to listen. Disagreement doesn't mean disrespect, and how you handle these moments can either strengthen or weaken the relationship.

1. *Choose Respect Over Confrontation.* When disagreements arise, prioritize respect and humility. Instead of confronting your pastor in a way that feels adversarial, express your concerns thoughtfully and privately. Your goal should be to seek understanding, not to win an argument. Approach the conversation with a posture of listening, and be open to hearing their perspective, even if it differs from yours. Sometimes, simply hearing your pastor's rationale can bring clarity and resolve the disagreement.

2. *Focus on the Mission.* When there's tension between your personal opinion and the pastor's direction, refocus on the church's mission. Ask yourself, "Is this disagreement affecting the overall mission of the church?" If the issue is minor and doesn't hinder the church's goals, it may be worth letting go. However, if the disagreement affects a key aspect of the church's mission or values, it's important to address it directly and with a spirit of collaboration.

3. *Seek Guidance From Trusted Mentors.* If you find yourself struggling with ongoing disagreements, seek counsel from trusted mentors or church leaders who can offer objective advice. Sometimes, talking through the situation with someone outside the immediate church staff can provide clarity and help you navigate the issue with wisdom.

LESSONS FROM DAVID AND SAUL

The relationship between David and King Saul offers valuable lessons on how to navigate leadership challenges with respect and grace. Though Saul became increasingly hostile toward David, even attempting to kill him out of jealousy, David consistently chose to honor Saul's position as the Lord's anointed king. David had multiple opportunities to harm Saul in retaliation, but he refrained, showing great restraint and respect for Saul's authority, even when it was difficult.

David's example teaches us the importance of respecting leadership, even when we don't agree with their decisions. By maintaining a posture of humility and honoring Saul's role, David modeled what it looks like to trust God's plan, even in the face of personal conflict. As church staff members, we can apply this lesson by choosing to respect our pastor's leadership, even when we face challenges or disagreements. Ultimately, God is the one who appoints leaders, and our role is to serve faithfully in the positions we've been called to.

REFLECTION QUESTIONS

1. How can you maintain a healthy balance between viewing your pastor as both a spiritual leader and your boss?

2. What are some practical steps you can take to nurture your relationship with your pastor, especially when conflicts arise?

3. How might the story of David and Saul influence your approach to disagreements with your pastor or church leadership?

MENTOR MOMENTS FOR CHAPTER 10
MY PASTOR IS MY BOSS!—
NAVIGATING A DUAL RELATIONSHIP

Objective—Help the new staff member navigate the unique relationship of working for a pastor who is also their spiritual leader, offering guidance on maintaining respect, setting boundaries, and fostering a healthy working relationship.

Session Title—Balancing Roles: Serving Under Your Pastor and Boss

Time Required—30–45 minutes

RECOGNIZING THE DUAL ROLE OF PASTOR AND BOSS

- **Mentor's Prompt**—"Working for your pastor is a unique situation. They're both your spiritual leader and your employer, which can make it challenging to balance personal respect with professional expectations. Let's discuss how you can approach this dual role with wisdom."

- **Questions to Consider**

  ° How do you feel about having your pastor also serve as your direct supervisor?

  ° Are there any aspects of this dual role that you find challenging or that raise questions?

NOTES

ESTABLISHING BOUNDARIES AND OPEN COMMUNICATION

- **Mentor's Insight**—"It's essential to establish healthy boundaries and open lines of communication to avoid misunderstandings and maintain respect. Let's go over how you can keep these boundaries while remaining receptive and respectful to your pastor."

- **Questions for Reflection**

  ° What boundaries do you think are important in balancing this dual relationship?

  ° How will you approach open, respectful communication, especially if you disagree with your pastor?

NOTES

HONORING AUTHORITY WHILE MAINTAINING PROFESSIONALISM

- **Mentor's Guidance**—"Your pastor is not only your boss but a figure of spiritual authority. Honoring their role, even during disagreements, is crucial. Let's discuss how you can respectfully express your opinions while staying supportive."

- **Discussion Points**

  ° How will you handle situations where you may disagree with your pastor's direction or decision?

  ° What strategies can you use to maintain professionalism, especially during challenging conversations?

NOTES

FINAL REFLECTION AND PRAYER

- **Mentor's Closing Thought**—"Serving under your pastor requires humility, respect, and wisdom. Take some time to pray for guidance as you work to build a healthy, balanced relationship that honors both the ministry and your own spiritual journey."

- **Closing Prayer**—"Lord, thank You for placing [staff member's name] under the leadership of their pastor. Help them to serve with respect and integrity, honoring both the role of boss and spiritual guide. Grant them wisdom in every interaction, and let their relationship be a source of growth and unity. In Jesus' name, Amen."

CHAPTER 11

CARRYING THE VISION— MAKING THE CHURCH'S MISSION YOURS

Working on church staff is more than just fulfilling a set of job duties; it's about embracing the vision of the church and helping to bring it to life. Every church has a unique mission, shaped by its history, congregation, and leadership, and as a staff member, you become a steward of that mission. Much like a supporting cast in a production, your role enhances and amplifies the story the church is telling, moving it forward in ways that impact the congregation and community.

Embracing the church's vision means making it your own, internalizing it, and finding ways to bring your personal strengths and gifts to support it. When you align your work with the church's mission, you serve with purpose, conviction, and a sense of shared responsibility. In this chapter, we'll explore how to connect with the church's vision, integrate your strengths, and carry the mission in a way that feels authentic to you.

UNDERSTANDING AND EMBRACING THE CHURCH'S VISION

The vision of a church is its heartbeat, the guiding purpose that shapes everything from Sunday services to community outreach. Some churches focus on missions, others on discipleship, and still others on community transformation or evangelism. Whatever the focus, the vision acts as a roadmap, directing the church's activities and goals. As a staff member, it's essential to understand this vision, as it will inform your work, inspire your efforts, and keep you grounded in purpose.

When you join a church staff, take time to learn the vision and ask questions about its origins, meaning, and application. Talk to the pastor, attend vision-casting meetings, or review church documents that outline the mission. Understanding the vision means more than memorizing a statement—it's about absorbing the church's heart for ministry. This knowledge will help you connect your own work to the bigger picture, allowing you to serve with a sense of alignment and purpose.

Example: Early in my ministry career, I worked with a church that was passionate about community outreach. Their vision was centered around being a place of healing and restoration, where everyone in the community could find hope. This vision didn't just shape our Sunday services; it influenced every decision we made from the small groups we offered to the way we designed our events. By embracing this vision, each staff member understood they were contributing to a ministry that was much bigger than their individual roles. This created a sense of unity and motivation, as we all felt connected to the church's purpose.

MAKING THE VISION YOURS

Once you understand the church's vision, the next step is making it personal. This doesn't mean changing the vision to suit your preferences; rather, it's about finding ways to engage with it that resonate with your strengths and passions. Ask yourself how your gifts can support the mission. How can you use your specific skills and strengths to bring the vision to life?

1. *Identify How Your Strengths Support the Vision.* Reflect on your unique strengths, spiritual gifts, and talents, and think about how they align with the church's mission. For instance, if you have the gift of teaching, perhaps you can help create discipleship programs that nurture spiritual growth. If your strength is organization, you might take on a role in administration, making sure events and initiatives run smoothly. Each role has a place within the mission, and understanding where your strengths fit allows you to contribute meaningfully.

2. *Find Ways to Engage Beyond Your Role.* Embracing the vision means going beyond a job description when possible. Look for opportunities to engage with the church's mission in different ways. Volunteer for a ministry event, offer to lead a workshop, or take on a project that aligns with your gifts and the church's needs. When you invest yourself fully, you're not just filling a position—you're living out a calling that enriches the church's ministry.

3. *Develop Personal Goals Aligned With the Vision.* Setting personal goals that align with the church's vision keeps you motivated and focused. For example, if the church's mission is discipleship, set a goal to deepen your own study of the Bible, so you can share insights with others. Or, if the vision is outreach, challenge yourself to build relationships with commu-

nity members. Personal goals help you stay engaged and connected to the mission, bringing fresh energy and perspective
to your work.

4. *Stay Flexible and Open to New Ideas.* As a church staff member, your work will often require flexibility, as ministry needs
change and grow. Being open to new ideas and ways of serving allows you to carry the vision forward with a willingness
to adapt. When challenges arise or the church's direction
shifts, approach these moments with an attitude of learning
and growth. This flexibility reflects a deep commitment to the
mission and helps keep the ministry relevant and impactful.

THE POWER OF COLLECTIVE VISION

When each staff member embraces the church's vision, it creates a sense of collective purpose that strengthens the entire ministry.
Imagine a team where each person is using their strengths and talents to support a shared mission—it's a powerful and unifying force.
This collective vision is what sustains a ministry through challenges,
keeps the church focused on its goals, and ultimately creates lasting
impact in the congregation and community.

Serving in ministry can sometimes feel isolating, especially when
the work becomes challenging. But when you're part of a team that's
united in vision, you have the support, encouragement, and camara-
derie needed to push through. Knowing that you're not alone—that
others are equally committed to the mission—gives you resilience
and helps you carry the vision with joy, even in difficult times.

CARRYING THE VISION THROUGH YOUR WORK

Once you've internalized the church's vision, look for ways to embody it in your daily work. Think of each task as a small step toward a larger goal, one that contributes to the church's overall impact. Whether you're coordinating an event, teaching a class, or organizing logistics, each effort is an opportunity to reflect the church's mission.

Example: In one of my roles, we had a church staff team meeting every week, where we'd start by revisiting our mission statement and sharing updates on how each of our ministries was contributing to it. These meetings reminded us that our individual roles weren't just isolated tasks; they were part of a greater vision. By focusing on our collective mission, each staff member felt a renewed sense of purpose and responsibility, which was reflected in the work we did that week.

Embracing the vision is about being fully invested in the church's mission, so it flows through everything you do. When you approach your work as an extension of the church's vision, even the most routine tasks become meaningful. You're no longer just completing a to-do list; you're actively contributing to the kingdom of God.

FINAL THOUGHTS ON CARRYING THE VISION

Being part of the church's supporting cast means carrying the vision forward in ways that are both purposeful and personal. The church's mission becomes yours, and your strengths, gifts, and passions play a vital role in bringing it to life. By connecting with the vision, investing your whole self, and supporting the work of the entire team, you're contributing to something far greater than yourself.

As you continue in your role, remember that carrying the vision isn't about perfection; it's about faithfulness. It's about showing up, staying committed, and giving your best to serve the mission God has placed on your heart.

REFLECTION QUESTIONS

1. What aspects of the church's vision resonate most deeply with you, and how can you incorporate them into your daily work?

2. In what ways can you use your strengths and gifts to actively support the church's mission?

3. Think about a recent challenge or change in your role. How might embracing flexibility help you carry the vision more effectively?

MENTOR MOMENTS FOR CHAPTER 11
CARRYING THE VISION—MAKING THE CHURCH'S MISSION YOURS

Objective—Guide the new staff member in embracing and supporting the church's vision and mission, helping them connect personally to the church's goals and find ways to contribute meaningfully to its success.

Session Title—Aligning Your Heart: Embracing and Supporting the Church's Vision

Time Required—30–45 minutes

UNDERSTANDING AND EMBRACING THE CHURCH'S MISSION

- **Mentor's Prompt**—"Our church has a unique mission and purpose that guides everything we do. Understanding and embracing this vision is key to fulfilling your role. Let's discuss the church's mission and how you connect with it personally."

- **Questions to Consider**

  ° What resonates most with you about our church's vision and mission?

  ° How do you see your role supporting this vision, and what impact do you hope to make?

NOTES

CONNECTING PERSONAL GOALS WITH THE CHURCH'S VISION

- **Mentor's Insight**—"Your personal gifts, goals, and passions can enrich the church's mission in meaningful ways. Let's talk about how you can align your own goals with the church's vision to serve with purpose and enthusiasm."

- **Questions for Reflection**

    ° What are some specific ways you can use your strengths to support the church's mission?

    ° How can you integrate your personal goals with the church's broader vision to create a sense of fulfillment?

NOTES

STAYING COMMITTED THROUGH CHALLENGES

- **Mentor's Guidance**—"Working toward a common vision requires perseverance, especially during challenging times. Let's discuss ways you can stay committed to the church's mission and how you can remind yourself of its importance when challenges arise."

- **Discussion Points**

    ° How will you stay focused on the church's mission when faced with obstacles or frustrations?

    ° What practices or reminders can help you stay connected to the church's vision, especially during challenging seasons?

NOTES

FINAL REFLECTION AND PRAYER

- **Mentor's Closing Thought**—"Embracing and carrying the vision of the church is an honor and a responsibility. Take some time to pray for a heart that aligns with this mission, and for strength to contribute to it faithfully."

- **Closing Prayer**—"Lord, thank You for entrusting [staff member's name] with this part of Your mission. Help them to serve with passion, dedication, and humility as they carry the vision of this church. Strengthen them to overcome challenges, and may their work bring Your vision to life in our community. In Jesus' name, Amen."

CHAPTER 12

COMPENSATION AND NEGOTIATING SALARY IN MINISTRY

One of the most difficult conversations for many people entering church staff positions is the topic of compensation. Unlike corporate jobs where salary is often negotiable and based on market trends, ministry work often comes with limited financial resources due to the non-profit nature of most churches. However, this doesn't mean that compensation shouldn't be fair, or that you should undersell your own value.

While it's important to recognize the financial constraints that many churches face, it's equally important to know your worth, stay informed about market trends, and approach salary negotiations with confidence. In this chapter, we'll explore how to navigate the often-delicate issue of compensation, using data from sources like the Vanderbloemen Search Group's 2024 salary guide. We'll also discuss the importance of being a financial supporter of your church, whether through tithing or offering, and how to align financial expectations with your sense of calling.

UNDERSTANDING CHURCH COMPENSATION

Church staff compensation can vary widely depending on the size of the church, its location, and its financial health. According to the 2024 Vanderbloemen Church Compensation Report, salaries for non-pastoral roles range from moderate to competitive depending on the church's budget. For example, executive pastors in large churches (with over 2,000 attendees) may earn a salary that's comparable to that of mid-level managers in the corporate world, while administrative assistants or youth ministry directors may earn more modest incomes.

The report notes that church compensation is usually broken down by church size. Here are a few examples:

- *Small churches (under 500 attendees):* Compensation tends to be lower, with youth pastors, administrative staff, and worship leaders typically earning between $30,000 and $50,000 annually.

- *Mid-sized churches (500–1,999 attendees):* Salaries for ministry staff can range from $40,000 to $80,000 depending on the role and location.

- *Large churches (2,000+ attendees):* Executive-level roles, like directors of operations or campus pastors, can earn six-figure salaries, while other staff members, like communications directors or small group leaders, may earn between $60,000 and $90,000 annually.

It's important to understand that churches with larger congregations generally have more financial resources to allocate toward staff salaries, while smaller churches often have tighter budgets. That said, compensation should always reflect the responsibilities of the role and the value the staff member brings to the church.

NEGOTIATING SALARY IN MINISTRY

Negotiating salary in ministry can feel uncomfortable, especially since many people enter church work with a heart for service rather than financial gain. However, it's essential to approach these conversations with both transparency and professionalism. Being informed about salary trends for your role will help you navigate these discussions with confidence.

1. *Do Your Research.* Before entering a salary negotiation, research the market rate for your role in churches of similar size and context. The Vanderbloemen salary guide is a valuable resource that provides data on compensation for various ministry roles based on church size, region, and job function. Being equipped with this information will give you a realistic understanding of what you can expect and ensure that your salary aligns with industry standards.

2. *Communicate Your Value.* When negotiating, focus on the value you bring to the church. Highlight your experience, skills, and the unique contributions you can make to the ministry. Church leadership will appreciate that you are not simply focused on numbers but on the impact you plan to make in the church community. Frame the conversation around how your role supports the church's mission and how fair compensation allows you to serve wholeheartedly without financial stress.

3. *Consider Benefits Beyond Salary.* Many churches, especially smaller ones, may not be able to offer competitive salaries, but

they often provide other benefits such as housing allowances, health insurance, retirement plans, or paid sabbaticals. Be open to discussing these additional benefits during negotiations, as they can significantly contribute to your overall compensation package. For example, housing allowances can be tax-free in certain situations, making them a valuable benefit for ministry staff.

4. *Maintain a Kingdom Perspective.* While salary is important, it's essential to maintain a kingdom perspective when entering these discussions. Ministry work is a calling, and while fair compensation allows you to care for your needs and your family, it's not the only measure of success.

Approach the conversation with humility and a willingness to serve, recognizing that the church's financial limitations are often real, and your heart for ministry will be central to your ongoing fulfillment in the role.

BALANCING FINANCIAL EXPECTATIONS WITH CHURCH REALITY

It's important to acknowledge that churches are non-profit organizations with limited financial resources. Unlike businesses that generate revenue through sales, churches rely on tithes and offerings to support their operations, ministries, and staff salaries. As such, financial constraints are often a reality, especially in smaller congregations. This means that while it's crucial to advocate for fair compensation, it's equally important to recognize the church's financial limitations and be flexible when necessary.

That said, your compensation should reflect the scope of your responsibilities. If you find that your workload or job description has significantly expanded over time, it's appropriate to revisit the topic of compensation with your leadership. Open and respectful conversations about salary are not only fair but necessary to ensure you are compensated for the value you bring to the church.

SUPPORTING THE CHURCH FINANCIALLY

In addition to receiving compensation, it's important to remember that as a staff member, you are also a member of the church body. Many churches encourage staff to tithe or contribute financially to the church's mission, as a way of leading by example. Whether through a traditional tithe (10% of your income) or through offerings, contributing financially to the church is both a spiritual and practical commitment.

Supporting the church financially, even as a staff member, reflects your investment in the ministry and models generosity for the congregation. It's not just about the amount you give but about participating in the life of the church and demonstrating your belief in its mission.

REFLECTION QUESTIONS

1. How can you approach salary negotiations in ministry with both professionalism and a kingdom mindset?

2. What steps can you take to stay informed about market trends and ensure your compensation reflects your value?

3. How can you contribute to your church financially in a way that reflects your personal commitment to its mission?

MENTOR MOMENTS FOR CHAPTER 12
COMPENSATION AND NEGOTIATING SALARY IN MINISTRY

Objective—Guide the new staff member in understanding fair compensation practices within the context of church ministry, equipping them to discuss salary with confidence and align their financial expectations with their values and the church's resources.

Session Title—Honoring Your Value: Navigating Compensation with Integrity

Time Required—30–45 minutes

UNDERSTANDING THE BALANCE BETWEEN CALLING AND COMPENSATION

- **Mentor's Prompt**—"Working in ministry often involves balancing a sense of calling with practical financial needs. Let's discuss how compensation in church roles might differ from other fields and how you can approach it with a healthy perspective."

- **Questions to Consider**

  ° How do you view the relationship between calling and compensation in ministry?

  ° Are there any financial goals or needs you would like to discuss to ensure a sustainable balance?

NOTES

KNOWING YOUR WORTH AND NEGOTIATING RESPECTFULLY

- **Mentor's Insight**—"While ministry isn't always about money, it's important to recognize and advocate for your worth. Let's talk about how you can approach compensation discussions confidently and respectfully, while being mindful of the church's resources."

- **Questions for Reflection**

  ° What aspects of your role do you feel most contribute to your sense of worth in this position?

  ° How comfortable do you feel discussing compensation, and is there anything you'd like to know about the process?

NOTES

SUPPORTING THE CHURCH FINANCIALLY AND BUILDING TRUST

- **Mentor's Guidance**—"Giving back to the church is often part of ministry life. Whether through tithing or other contributions, supporting the church financially can deepen your connection and trust in its mission. Let's talk about how you see this aspect of ministry."

- **Discussion Points**

  ° How do you view financial contributions or tithing as part of your role in ministry?

  ° Are there ways you'd like to contribute to the church's mission that go beyond compensation?

NOTES

FINAL REFLECTION AND PRAYER

- **Mentor's Closing Thought**—"Compensation is a part of ministry that requires trust, respect, and an understanding of the church's mission. Pray for God's guidance as you navigate this area with integrity, ensuring both your needs and the church's values are honored."

- **Closing Prayer**—"Lord, thank You for providing for [staff member's name] and for the opportunity to serve in this ministry. Guide them in navigating their compensation with wisdom and humility, trusting You to meet every need. Help them to honor both their value and the church's mission. In Jesus' name, Amen."

CHAPTER 13

LEADING WITH PURPOSE AND INFLUENCE

Leadership on church staff is about more than holding a position; it's about serving with purpose, humility, and a genuine commitment to God's people. In a ministry setting, influence isn't built through titles or authority but through relationships, trust, and a consistent example of servant leadership. Jesus demonstrated this in His own ministry, leading by washing His disciples' feet, teaching through service, and showing compassion in all He did. In the same way, church staff members are called to lead not by power, but by purpose and a heart to serve.

This chapter explores what it means to lead with purpose, cultivate influence, and embody servant leadership within the church. Whether you're a pastoral staff member, a worship leader, or an administrative team member, understanding your influence and using it wisely can create a culture of unity and respect that strengthens the entire church body.

THE FOUNDATION OF SERVANT LEADERSHIP

Servant leadership is central to Christian ministry and involves leading by putting others first. Jesus set the ultimate example of this by showing love, humility, and sacrifice in all He did. In Mark 10:45, He said, "For even the Son of Man did not come to be served, but to serve, and to give his life as a ransom for many." This form of leadership stands in contrast to the world's view of power and authority, as it prioritizes service, compassion, and humility over status.

As church staff, adopting a servant leadership mindset means being willing to do whatever is necessary to serve the church, whether or not it aligns with your job description. It might mean stepping into an unfamiliar role when needed, staying late to support an event, or simply being present for others in their times of need. Servant leadership is not always glamorous, but it is profoundly impactful, building trust and respect that amplifies your influence within the church.

Example: I once worked with a facilities manager named Jim who had an incredible servant's heart. Although his primary role was maintenance, he often went above and beyond, helping with events, setting up chairs, and even greeting congregants when he saw a need. Jim's humble willingness to serve created a culture of kindness and respect, and his influence extended far beyond his official role. Jim reminded everyone of the power of serving without seeking recognition, embodying the heart of a true servant leader.

BUILDING INFLUENCE THROUGH TRUST AND CONSISTENCY

Influence in ministry doesn't come from a title; it comes from trust. Trust is earned over time through consistency, integrity, and a commitment to others' well-being. People look to church staff members for guidance, stability, and support, and your ability to influence others is directly tied to how well you live out these values.

1. *Be Consistent in Character and Actions.* Consistency is crucial for building trust. Whether it's showing up on time, following through on commitments, or treating people with kindness, consistent actions reinforce your reliability. This trustworthiness makes people feel comfortable seeking your guidance and support, knowing they can count on you.

2. *Cultivate Transparency and Integrity.* In ministry, integrity is everything. Being transparent about decisions, open to feedback, and honest in all interactions helps create an environment where people feel respected and valued. Integrity isn't about perfection—it's about owning mistakes, being accountable, and striving to do what's right. This creates a foundation of trust that strengthens your influence.

INVEST IN RELATIONSHIPS

Relationships are at the heart of ministry and taking time to build meaningful connections shows people you genuinely care about them. Be approachable, listen actively, and take an interest in people's lives outside of church. Building relationships isn't just about networking; it's about fostering a sense of community where everyone feels valued. When people feel known and appreciated, they are more open to your influence and guidance.

LEADING WITH VISION AND PURPOSE

Effective leadership in ministry requires clarity of vision and a deep sense of purpose. As a church staff member, you're entrusted with helping carry out the church's mission, which means leading with intentionality and alignment to that mission. People follow leaders who have a clear sense of direction and who communicate that direction with purpose.

1. *Align Your Role With the Church's Vision.* Every staff member plays a role in advancing the church's mission. Take time to understand how your work aligns with the church's vision and communicate that alignment to others. When people see that your actions are intentional and connected to a larger purpose, they are more likely to support and trust your leadership.

2. *Communicate Vision Clearly and Consistently.* Sharing the vision isn't just the job of the lead pastor; every staff member can contribute by reinforcing the church's goals in their own areas of influence. Be intentional about reminding your team and volunteers of the purpose behind their work. This creates a sense of shared mission that inspires and motivates others to stay committed, even when challenges arise.

3. *Set an Example of Purpose-Driven Service.* Leading by example means embodying the church's values and showing others what it looks like to serve with purpose. When people see you serving wholeheartedly, they are inspired to follow suit. Set an example by approaching your work with joy, dedication, and a positive attitude, showing others that every role, no matter how small, contributes to the greater mission.

LEADING THROUGH CHALLENGES WITH GRACE

Leadership is often tested during times of difficulty, and ministry is no exception. Whether facing a personal challenge, a disagreement within the team, or a difficult season for the church, how you handle these situations will impact your influence. Leading through challenges requires resilience, empathy, and a willingness to seek unity.

1. *Approach Conflict With an Open Mind and Heart.* In church leadership, conflict is inevitable. Differences in opinion, misunderstandings, or unmet expectations can arise, but handling these situations with grace can strengthen rather than harm relationships. Approach conflicts with a desire for resolution, listening to others' perspectives, and seeking common ground. This approach not only helps resolve issues but also demonstrates humility and respect.

2. *Be a Source of Stability.* In challenging times, people look to leaders for reassurance and guidance. Be a steady presence, showing others that you can face adversity with faith and calm. Stability doesn't mean suppressing your emotions; it means choosing to respond with wisdom and care. When people see you handling challenges with grace, they feel more secure and supported, knowing they can rely on you.

3. *Encourage a Culture of Support.* Leading through challenges isn't something you do alone. Encourage a culture of support within your team, where people feel comfortable sharing burdens, seeking help, and offering encouragement. A supportive environment strengthens the entire team and shows that leadership in the church isn't about hierarchy—it's about mutual respect and partnership.

REFLECTION QUESTIONS

1. In what ways can you embody servant leadership in your role, both in public and behind the scenes?

2. How can you build trust within your team and congregation through consistency and integrity?

3. Think about a recent challenge in ministry. How might you lead through future challenges with grace and purpose?

MENTOR MOMENTS FOR CHAPTER 13 LEADING WITH PURPOSE AND INFLUENCE

Objective—Guide the new staff member in developing their leadership skills and using their influence positively within the church setting, regardless of their formal position.

Session Title—Empowering Others: Leading With Purpose and Influence

Time Required—30–45 minutes

UNDERSTANDING LEADERSHIP AS SERVICE

- **Mentor's Prompt**—"Leadership in the church is about serving others, not just directing them. Let's discuss how you can embrace a servant leadership mindset that focuses on empowering and uplifting others."

- **Questions to Consider**

  ° How do you view the role of a leader in a church setting?

  ° What qualities do you feel are essential to lead effectively in ministry?

NOTES

BUILDING INFLUENCE THROUGH RELATIONSHIPS

- **Mentor's Insight**—"Influence isn't about authority; it's about building trust and strong relationships. Let's talk about ways you can cultivate influence by fostering genuine connections with team members and congregants."

- **Questions for Reflection**
  - ° What steps can you take to build trust and connection with those you work with?

  - ° Are there specific ways you hope to positively influence the church culture?

NOTES

MAINTAINING INTEGRITY IN LEADERSHIP

- **Mentor's Guidance**—"Integrity is foundational to effective leadership, especially in ministry. Let's discuss how you can remain true to your values and God's calling as you lead and influence others."

- **Discussion Points**
  - ° How do you plan to ensure integrity and consistency in your actions?

  - ° Are there challenges you anticipate in maintaining integrity, and how can we address them?

NOTES

FINAL REFLECTION AND PRAYER

- **Mentor's Closing Thought**—"Leading in ministry is an opportunity to make a meaningful impact. Pray for guidance, wisdom, and a heart that leads with humility and purpose."

- **Closing Prayer**—"Lord, thank You for giving [staff member's name] the opportunity to lead and influence others. Help them to serve with integrity, humility, and a genuine love for Your people. May their leadership bring glory to You and strengthen Your church. In Jesus' name, Amen."

CHAPTER 14

ON CALL 24/7—MANAGING TIME EXPECTATIONS

Church staff positions are unlike any other job. In most work-places, you clock in at a set time and leave at the end of the day, your responsibilities neatly compartmentalized into work hours. But in ministry, the lines between personal time and work time are often blurred. Church staff members are frequently on call, whether that's attending to the needs of the congregation, planning last-minute events, or providing spiritual care in emergencies. There's an unspoken reality in many churches that staff members are available 24/7, regardless of whether it's sustainable, ethical, or even legal.

This expectation can be overwhelming, and without clear boundaries, it's easy to experience burnout, frustration, and a loss of balance between work and personal life. However, managing these expectations is crucial not only for your well-being but also for your ability to serve the church effectively in the long term. In this chapter, we'll explore how to navigate these demands, set healthy boundaries, and manage the often-unspoken expectation of being on call in ministry.

UNDERSTANDING THE UNSPOKEN REALITY

The expectation to be always available is something many church staff members experience but rarely talk about openly. Congregants might assume that because you work for the church, you're always ready to respond to a need—whether it's an emergency hospital visit, a late-night phone call, or organizing an event at the last minute. While ministry does often require flexibility, it's important to recognize that constant availability is not sustainable for anyone.

In many cases, this 24/7 expectation is an unspoken part of the church culture, something that has evolved over time rather than being clearly defined. Understanding this reality allows you to approach your role with clarity and intention, acknowledging the need for flexibility while also protecting your own well-being.

SETTING HEALTHY BOUNDARIES

Healthy boundaries are essential to sustaining a long-term career in ministry. While there will be seasons when extra time and energy are required, it's important to communicate your own limitations and ensure that your work doesn't consume every aspect of your life. Setting boundaries doesn't mean shirking responsibility; it means creating space to recharge so you can continue serving effectively.

1. *Communicate Your Availability.* One of the most effective ways to manage expectations is by clearly communicating your availability. If your church doesn't have a formal policy on staff hours, create one for yourself and discuss it with your supervisor. Let people know when you are available and when you need personal time. For example, you might set certain hours for non-emergencies, ensuring that evenings and weekends are reserved for your family unless an urgent need arises.

2. *Establish Personal Time for Rest and Renewal.* Ministry work is emotionally and spiritually draining, which makes it crucial to carve out time for rest and renewal. Make it a priority to schedule regular time off, including vacations, sabbaticals, or weekly days of rest where you can step away from work. This time will allow you to recharge and maintain your spiritual health, which is essential for serving others well.

3. *Learn to Say "No" With Grace.* In ministry, it can feel difficult to say "no" when a congregant asks for help, even if it's outside of your work hours or responsibilities. However, learning to say "no" with grace is essential for maintaining balance. It's okay to let people know when you aren't available and to direct them to other resources or staff members if necessary. Saying no doesn't mean you're unwilling to help—it means you're managing your time and energy wisely.

MANAGING CONGREGATIONAL EXPECTATIONS

The expectations of the congregation can often contribute to the feeling of being on call 24/7. Many people assume that because you work for the church, you're available at all times for any issue they might have. While it's important to be accessible and responsive, it's equally important to manage these expectations realistically.

1. *Set Clear Boundaries With Congregants.* Just as you communicate your availability to your supervisor, it's important to set clear boundaries with congregants. Let people know when they can expect a response from you and when they should reach out to other staff members. For example, you might establish that non-urgent emails will be answered within 24–48 hours or that you are available for emergency pastoral care during certain hours.

2. *Create a Team-Based Approach to Care.* One way to reduce the pressure of being on call all the time is to create a team-based approach to pastoral care and ministry needs. Encourage the congregation to reach out to other staff members or volunteers when appropriate, rather than relying solely on you for every issue. This not only spreads the workload but also empowers others in the church to take on leadership roles.

3. *Educate the Congregation About Boundaries.* Many congregants may not even realize the toll that 24/7 availability takes on church staff. Take opportunities to educate the congregation about the importance of boundaries, rest, and self-care for ministry leaders. This can be done through sermons, church newsletters, or casual conversations. Helping people understand that staff members need personal time too can foster a healthier church culture where boundaries are respected.

BALANCING MINISTRY AND PERSONAL LIFE

Perhaps the greatest challenge of being on call in ministry is maintaining a healthy balance between work and personal life. Ministry often requires a deep emotional and spiritual investment, and when boundaries are not in place, it can begin to consume every aspect of your life. Balancing these demands means finding practical ways to prioritize your personal well-being while still serving the church effectively.

Protect Your Family Time. Family time is often the first thing to suffer when ministry work becomes overwhelming. Protecting your family time is crucial not only for your relationships but also for your mental and emotional health. Set specific times during the week that are reserved for your family and make them non-negotiable. Let your church know when you're unavailable due to family commitments and ensure that your family feels valued and supported.

Establish a Support Network. Having a support network outside of the church is invaluable for maintaining balance. This might include friends, mentors, or colleagues in ministry who understand the unique pressures you face. These relationships provide a safe space to vent frustrations, seek advice, and receive encouragement. Surrounding yourself with people who can support you personally helps you stay grounded, even when the demands of ministry feel overwhelming.

Regularly Evaluate Your Work-Life Balance. Work-life balance isn't something you set once and forget. It requires regular evaluation and adjustment as seasons change. Take time to reflect on your current balance and ask yourself whether your boundaries are being respected. If you find that your personal time is being consistently interrupted or that you're feeling burned out, it may be time to revisit the boundaries you've set and make adjustments.

REFLECTION QUESTIONS

1. How can you set healthier boundaries in your ministry role to protect your time and well-being?

2. What steps can you take to communicate your availability and manage congregational expectations more effectively?

3. In what ways can you ensure that your family time is prioritized, even in the midst of a demanding ministry schedule?

MENTOR MOMENTS FOR CHAPTER 14 ON CALL 24/7—MANAGING TIME EXPECTATIONS

Objective—Help the new staff member understand and navigate the unique time demands of ministry, setting healthy boundaries while staying responsive to the needs of the church.

Session Title—Balancing Service and Self-Care: Navigating Time Demands in Ministry

Time Required—30–45 minutes

UNDERSTANDING THE NATURE OF ON-CALL MINISTRY

- **Mentor's Prompt**—"Ministry work often involves being available outside of typical hours, especially during emergencies. Let's discuss what it means to be on call and how you can balance these demands with personal needs."

- **Questions to Consider**

  ° How do you feel about being available beyond regular work hours?

  ° Are there any concerns or questions you have about handling on-call situations?

NOTES

SETTING BOUNDARIES TO MAINTAIN BALANCE

- **Mentor's Insight**—"Even in ministry, setting boundaries is essential to avoid burnout. Let's talk about strategies for balancing availability with the need for rest and time with loved ones."

- **Questions for Reflection**
  - ° What boundaries would help you maintain a healthy balance?
  - ° How can you communicate these boundaries effectively with your team and church members?

NOTES

PRIORITIZING SELF-CARE AND PERSONAL TIME

- **Mentor's Guidance**—"Making time for self-care doesn't mean neglecting your role; it means ensuring you're at your best to serve. Let's discuss practical ways to incorporate rest and renewal into your routine."

- **Discussion Points**
  - ° What activities or practices help you recharge spiritually and emotionally?
  - ° How can you commit to regular self-care while meeting the demands of your role?

NOTES

FINAL REFLECTION AND PRAYER

- **Mentor's Closing Thought**—"Balancing time commitments in ministry requires wisdom and self-awareness. Take a moment to pray for strength, balance, and guidance as you serve and care for yourself."

- **Closing Prayer**—"Lord, thank You for [staff member's name] and their dedication to serving. Help them to find a healthy balance between their calling and personal needs. Give them wisdom in setting boundaries and resilience in their service. In Jesus' name, Amen."

CHAPTER 15

BALANCING LIFE, STAFF, AND FAMILY COMMITMENTS

Ministry work is a calling, but it doesn't come without challenges—especially when it comes to balancing the demands of church staff life with personal and family commitments. The work of the church often requires long hours, late-night meetings, and weekend events, all of which can take a toll on your personal time and family relationships. For those with families, this balance is even more delicate, as your role in the church intersects with your role at home.

In my years on church staff, I've seen families thrive in ministry settings, and I've also seen families struggle under the weight of unrealistic expectations. Some churches deeply value and prioritize staff members' family lives, making room for rest and personal time, while others may, intentionally or unintentionally, create an environment where work takes precedence over everything else. Navigating this dynamic well requires intentionality, clear communication, and a commitment to maintaining healthy boundaries between ministry and family life.

In this chapter, we'll explore strategies for balancing your church staff responsibilities with your family commitments, the importance of knowing the church's culture when it comes to family values, and practical ways to thrive in both your ministry and home life.

UNDERSTANDING THE CHURCH'S CULTURE REGARDING FAMILY LIFE

Each church has a unique culture when it comes to balancing staff responsibilities and personal life. Some churches explicitly encourage staff to prioritize family and build rest into their schedules, while others may implicitly expect staff members to be available 24/7 without regard for personal time. It's essential to understand where your church falls on this spectrum and to evaluate how well it aligns with your family's needs.

Example: In one church I consulted with, family was a central value of the ministry. The leadership made it clear that staff members should prioritize time with their families, even if it meant occasionally missing a meeting or event. This created a culture of mutual respect, where staff felt supported both at work and at home. In contrast, I've also seen churches where the demands of ministry were relentless, and staff members felt constant pressure to put work first, often leading to burnout and strained family relationships.

As you consider joining or continuing on church staff, ask specific questions about the church's expectations regarding family life. Do they value time with family, or do they expect you to be at every event, regardless of personal commitments? Understanding the church's culture will help you navigate your role more effectively and ensure that you can maintain a healthy balance.

COMMUNICATING BOUNDARIES WITH YOUR CHURCH

Setting and communicating clear boundaries with your church leadership is one of the most important steps in balancing ministry work with family commitments. Boundaries are not about shirking responsibility; rather, they are about protecting both your ability to serve the church well and your capacity to nurture your family relationships. When you set healthy boundaries, you're ensuring that you have the emotional and physical energy to give your best to both your ministry and your family.

1. Have Open Conversations With Your Supervisor. Early in your tenure, or as soon as it becomes necessary, sit down with your supervisor to discuss your family commitments and any potential conflicts with church responsibilities. Share your desire to serve the church with excellence while also maintaining a healthy family life. Most leaders will appreciate your honesty and be willing to work with you to create a schedule that supports both.

2. Be Clear About Your Availability. While there will always be emergencies in ministry, it's important to establish clear expectations about your general availability. Let your supervisor know if there are specific times you need to protect for family commitments, such as evenings or weekends, and be proactive in creating a balance that works for both you and the church. Being transparent about your needs can help prevent misunderstandings down the line.

3. Involve Your Family in the Process. Family dynamics are an essential part of ministry work. If your church allows it, consider involving your family in your ministry when appropriate. This could mean attending church events together or involving your spouse or children in volunteering opportuni-

ties. While it's important to maintain boundaries, integrating your family into the church's life can foster a sense of community and shared purpose.

SETTING BOUNDARIES AT HOME

While setting boundaries with the church is important, it's equally essential to set boundaries at home. Ministry work can be all-consuming, and without clear boundaries, it's easy for work to seep into every part of your life, causing strain in your family relationships.

1. *Create Sacred Family Time.* Just as you protect your time at church, you need to protect time with your family. Set aside specific times during the week for family activities and make these times non-negotiable. Whether it's a weekly family dinner, a movie night, or a day of rest, creating sacred family time helps ensure that your loved ones feel prioritized, even in the midst of a busy ministry schedule.

2. *Turn Off the Work When You're at Home.* Ministry often involves late-night phone calls, urgent meetings, and last-minute crises, but it's important to create boundaries around work when you're at home. Set a rule to turn off your phone or work email during family time and resist the urge to let work-related stress dominate your conversations at home. Protecting your family's emotional space allows you to recharge and return to ministry with a refreshed perspective.

3. *Don't Be Afraid to Delegate.* One of the biggest challenges in ministry is the feeling that everything falls on your shoulders. However, delegation is key to maintaining balance. Trust your team and volunteers to take on responsibilities when needed, and don't hesitate to ask for help if you're feeling

overwhelmed. A healthy ministry is built on collaboration, not overburdening any one person.

THRIVING IN BOTH MINISTRY AND FAMILY LIFE

Balancing ministry and family life is not about compartmentalizing one over the other, but about creating harmony between the two. It's about being present where you are—fully engaged at church when you're serving, and fully present at home when you're with your family. Thriving in both areas requires intentionality, communication, and a willingness to adapt when necessary.

Example: One pastor I knew made it a point to spend every Friday with his wife and children, no matter what was happening at the church. He communicated this clearly with his leadership team and congregation, and as a result, his family thrived, and he was able to bring his full energy to the church when he was working. I cannot stress to you enough, put your family first. Your position at the church will eventually be filled by someone else but no one can replace your role in your family.

When you prioritize both your family and your ministry, you not only model healthy boundaries for your congregation but also demonstrate that your family is part of your ministry. By showing that it's possible to honor both commitments, you're setting an example for others who may also be struggling to find balance in their lives.

REFLECTION QUESTIONS

1. What steps can you take to better understand your church's culture around family commitments and personal time?

2. How can you communicate your boundaries effectively with church leadership and congregants to ensure your family is prioritized?

3. What practical strategies can you implement to protect sacred family time and create a healthy balance between ministry and personal life?

MENTOR MOMENTS FOR CHAPTER 15
BALANCING LIFE, STAFF, AND FAMILY COMMITMENTS

Objective—Support the new staff member in managing the demands of ministry alongside family responsibilities, helping them maintain healthy relationships and prioritize family commitments.

Session Title—Serving With Balance: Prioritizing Family While in Ministry

Time Required—30–45 minutes

RECOGNIZING THE IMPORTANCE OF FAMILY PRIORITIES

- **Mentor's Prompt**—"Your family is a vital part of your ministry. Serving well means finding a balance that honors both your work and family life. Let's talk about ways to ensure your family commitments are prioritized alongside your ministry responsibilities."

- **Questions to Consider**
  - What are your personal priorities when it comes to family and ministry balance?
  - Are there specific challenges you anticipate in managing these commitments?

NOTES

SETTING BOUNDARIES TO PROTECT FAMILY TIME

- Mentor's Insight—"Setting boundaries around family time is essential to maintain healthy relationships and avoid burnout. Let's discuss strategies for protecting your family time without neglecting your ministry role."

- **Questions for Reflection**

  ° What boundaries can you set to ensure dedicated time for family?

  ° How will you communicate these boundaries to your team and congregation?

NOTES

INCLUDING FAMILY IN YOUR MINISTRY JOURNEY

- **Mentor's Guidance**—"Sometimes, involving your family in aspects of your ministry can strengthen both relationships and support your role. Let's explore ways to integrate family and ministry in ways that are meaningful and balanced."

- **Discussion Points**

  ° Are there ways your family can be involved in your ministry, and how can you ensure it's healthy for them?

  ° How can you encourage a supportive church culture that values family commitments?

NOTES

FINAL REFLECTION AND PRAYER

- Mentor's Closing Thought—"Balancing family and ministry requires intentional effort and prayer. Take time to ask for wisdom in managing both with love and dedication."

- Closing Prayer—"Lord, thank You for [staff member's name] and their commitment to both family and ministry. Give them wisdom to balance these priorities well and strength to serve both faithfully. May their family be blessed by their work and see Your love through them. In Jesus' name, Amen."

CHAPTER 16

KNOWING WHEN IT'S TIME TO LEAVE STAFF

Ministry work is often deeply fulfilling, but it can also be challenging. Sometimes, despite our best efforts, we reach a point where we begin to question whether we're still in the right place. Deciding to leave a church staff position is never an easy choice, but it's a reality that many church staff members face at some point in their career. The decision can be especially difficult when you're invested in the church's mission, have deep relationships with your team and congregants, or feel a strong sense of calling to ministry.

However, there are times when it's necessary to move on, either because the environment has become unhealthy or because God is leading you in a different direction. Recognizing the signs that it's time to leave, understanding how to make the transition with honor, and leaving with your relationships and integrity intact are all essential parts of navigating this difficult decision.

In this chapter, we'll explore the common reasons people leave ministry positions, the signs that it may be time to move on, and how to leave well when that time comes.

COMMON REASONS FOR LEAVING A MINISTRY ROLE

I conducted a brief survey with about 25 former church staff members. The survey revealed that while some leave for positive reasons, such as new opportunities or a change in calling, many leave due to negative experiences. The most frequently cited reasons include constant tension, a lack of appreciation for their expertise, and being forced into compromises that conflict with their integrity. Let's explore these in more detail.

1. *Constant Tension and Burnout.* Ministry work is demanding, and when the pressure becomes unrelenting, it can lead to emotional, physical, and spiritual burnout. Constant tension, whether due to leadership conflicts, unhealthy expectations, or unmanageable workloads, is often a major reason why people leave ministry. If you find yourself consistently feeling drained, anxious, or resentful about your role, it may be time to evaluate whether the job is sustainable for your well-being.

2. *Feeling Unvalued or Underutilized.* Many church staff members are highly skilled and bring unique gifts to the table, but sometimes they find themselves in roles that don't allow them to fully use their expertise. If your voice is not being heard, or you feel like your contributions are being overlooked or undervalued, it can lead to frustration and a sense of being underutilized. Ministry should be a place where your gifts are used to their fullest potential, and if you consistently feel sidelined, it might be time to consider moving on.

3. *Compromising Integrity or Personal Values.* In some cases, staff members are asked to make compromises that conflict with their values or integrity. This might involve being pressured to participate in decisions or actions that go against your conscience or biblical principles. When your integrity

is at stake, it's crucial to evaluate whether you can continue serving in a role that requires such compromises. Integrity in ministry is non-negotiable and protecting it may mean stepping away from a toxic environment.

4. *Stagnant Leadership or Vision.* A lack of leadership growth or vision can create an environment where staff members feel stifled or stuck. When leaders fail to inspire, adapt, or cast a compelling vision, the ministry can stagnate, leaving staff frustrated and disengaged. If you find yourself feeling like the church's mission or leadership is no longer moving forward, it may be time to evaluate whether God is calling you to serve elsewhere.

SIGNS IT'S TIME TO LEAVE

Deciding to leave a church job is rarely clear-cut, but there are signs that can help you discern when it's time to move on. Some key indicators include:

1. *Emotional and Spiritual Burnout.* If you are consistently feeling drained, anxious, or spiritually dry, and if no amount of rest or sabbatical time seems to help, it may be a sign that you are experiencing deep burnout. While burnout can often be resolved with rest or a change in workload, if the emotional and spiritual toll becomes overwhelming, it may be time to consider leaving.

2. *Feeling Unused or Undervalued.* If your gifts and skills are not being used, or you find yourself constantly feeling like your contributions don't matter, it may be a sign that the church is not the right fit for your ministry. Feeling unappreciated or sidelined can lead to resentment and frustration, which can affect both your work and your spiritual life.

3. *Ongoing Leadership Conflicts.* While conflict is natural in any organization, unresolved or ongoing conflicts with leadership can create a toxic environment that hinders your ability to serve effectively. If attempts to resolve these conflicts have failed, and the situation continues to cause stress or tension, it may be time to move on.

4. *Loss of Passion for the Mission.* If you no longer feel connected to the church's mission or vision, it can be difficult to serve with the same enthusiasm and energy. Ministry is a deeply personal calling, and if the mission no longer resonates with your heart, it's worth considering whether God is calling you to a new season of ministry elsewhere.

LEAVING WITH CLARITY AND HONOR

When it becomes clear that it's time to leave, it's important to do so with clarity, honor, and respect for the church, its leadership, and its mission. Here are some key steps to take:

1. *Pray for Discernment.* Leaving a ministry role is a significant decision, and it should be made with careful prayer and discernment. Seek God's guidance and ask for clarity about whether He is calling you to a new season of ministry. Take time to reflect on your reasons for leaving and ensure that your decision is rooted in prayerful consideration.

2. *Communicate Clearly and Respectfully.* When you decide to leave, communicate your decision clearly and respectfully to your pastor or supervisor. Be honest about your reasons but avoid blame or criticism. Frame the conversation around your personal journey and calling, rather than pointing fingers or highlighting frustrations. Honoring the leadership and main-

taining positive relationships will help ensure a smoother transition.

3. *Leave Relationships Intact.* One of the most important aspects of leaving a ministry job is maintaining your relationships. Even if the environment has been challenging, it's essential to leave with grace and to avoid speaking negatively about the church or its leadership. Keep your focus on the bigger picture—your commitment to God's work and the relationships you've built with those you've served.

4. *Speak Life About the Church.* When you leave, speak life about the church and its mission, even if your experience has been difficult. As a staff member, your words carry weight, and how you speak about the church as you transition will impact how others view both you and the ministry. By speaking positively about the church and its future, you honor the work you've done and the people you've served.

REFLECTION QUESTIONS

1. What are the key factors that might indicate it's time for you to leave your ministry position?

2. How can you navigate leaving a church job in a way that maintains honor, integrity, and positive relationships?

3. What steps can you take to ensure you leave your role with clarity and respect, even in challenging circumstances?

MENTOR MOMENTS FOR CHAPTER 16
KNOWING WHEN IT'S TIME TO LEAVE STAFF

Objective—Guide the new staff member in recognizing the signs that it might be time to transition from their current role and to help them approach this decision with clarity, grace, and wisdom.

Session Title—Discerning Your Next Step: When to Transition From Your Ministry Role

Time Required—30–45 minutes

RECOGNIZING THE SIGNS OF TRANSITION

- **Mentor's Prompt**—"Ministry is often seasonal and knowing when it's time to move on is important for both personal growth and the health of the church. Let's talk about some common signs that suggest it might be time to consider a transition."

- **Questions to Consider**

  ° Have you felt any consistent internal promptings or external factors that suggest it might be time to move on?

  ° How do you feel about the idea of transitioning out of your current role, and what concerns or hopes do you have?

NOTES

SEEKING CONFIRMATION THROUGH PRAYER AND COUNSEL

- **Mentor's Insight**—"Decisions like these should be approached prayerfully and with input from trusted advisors. Let's discuss how you can seek confirmation through prayer, Scripture, and wise counsel."

- **Questions for Reflection**

  ° What steps have you taken to seek God's direction in this area?

  ° Are there trusted mentors, friends, or spiritual leaders you can talk to for insight and support?

NOTES

PLANNING A GRACEFUL EXIT

- **Mentor's Guidance**—"Leaving a ministry role should be done with respect and thoughtfulness. Let's go over what it means to leave well, protecting relationships and ensuring a smooth transition for the team and church."

- **Discussion Points**

  ° What steps can you take to communicate your decision in a way that honors the church and your relationships?

  ° How will you ensure your responsibilities are handed over smoothly to minimize disruption?

NOTES

FINAL REFLECTION AND PRAYER

- **Mentor's Closing Thought**—"Transitioning out of a role is a significant step, and it's important to do so with peace and confidence. Take a moment to reflect on this possibility and ask God for His wisdom and guidance in your decision."

- **Closing Prayer**—"Lord, thank You for the time [staff member's name] has spent in this ministry. If You are calling them to a new season, give them clarity, peace, and courage to step forward. Help them to leave with grace and integrity, honoring the relationships and the work they have done. Guide their path and provide reassurance that You are with them in every step. In Jesus' name, Amen."

CHAPTER 17

THRIVING IN YOUR KINGDOM ASSIGNMENT

Working in ministry is more than just a job—it's a kingdom assignment. When you step into a church staff role, you are taking on the responsibility of helping to build God's kingdom through the local church. It's a deeply fulfilling calling, but it's also one that can be filled with challenges and pressures. The key to thriving in ministry is not just to survive the demands but to flourish in the work you've been given.

In this final chapter, we will revisit Carlie's story, which reminds us that thriving in ministry requires intentionality, self-awareness, and a supportive environment. We will also explore how church staff can maintain their passion for ministry, avoid burnout, and ensure that their light continues to shine brightly throughout their journey.

REVISITING CARLIE'S STORY

Carlie was excited when she first interviewed for the children's director role at her church. The interview committee loved her enthusiasm, creativity, and heart for children's ministry. They were convinced she was the perfect fit for the job, and she was thrilled to step into a full-time role in the church she loved. But despite all the initial excitement, I remember feeling hesitant to hire her. I saw the light in her eyes, the spark of someone who was ready to serve God with everything she had, and I didn't want that light to go out.

Two years later, that's exactly what happened. The demands of the role, the constant pressure, and the emotional weight of ministry had dimmed the light in Carlie's eyes. She was exhausted, overwhelmed, and struggling to keep up. The very work she once loved had become a burden she could no longer carry.

Carlie's story is one that's all too common in ministry. Passionate, gifted people join church staff with a heart to serve, only to find themselves burned out and discouraged within a few years. But it doesn't have to be this way. By being intentional about self-care, seeking support from others, and keeping their calling front and center, church staff can not only survive but thrive in their kingdom assignments.

KEEPING THE LIGHT SHINING

The demands of church work can sometimes make it easy to lose sight of why you started in the first place. Long hours, difficult situations, and the emotional toll of caring for others can weigh you down. But thriving in your ministry role means finding ways to keep the light shining, even when the road gets tough.

1. *Stay Connected to Your Calling.* One of the most important ways to thrive in ministry is to stay connected to your calling. Remember why you stepped into ministry in the first place and hold onto that sense of purpose. When the work gets hard, reconnecting with your calling can help you stay

focused and motivated. Make time for personal reflection, prayer, and spiritual growth to ensure that your relationship with God remains at the forefront of everything you do.

2. *Prioritize Rest and Renewal.* Ministry can be exhausting, especially if you don't take time to rest and renew your spirit. It's easy to feel like you always need to be available, but in reality, you can't serve others effectively if you're running on empty. Make rest a priority, whether that means taking regular days off, scheduling vacations, or simply setting aside time each week to recharge. Rest isn't just a luxury; it's a necessity for long-term success in ministry.

3. *Seek Support and Accountability.* No one thrives in ministry alone. Seek out mentors, peers, or spiritual advisors who can provide guidance, encouragement, and accountability. Whether it's a regular check-in with a mentor or a peer group of fellow staff members, having people who understand the challenges you face can be invaluable. These relationships will help you process your experiences, offer support during difficult seasons, and keep you grounded in your calling.

CREATING A HEALTHY MINISTRY ENVIRONMENT

For church staff to thrive, the church itself must foster a supportive and healthy environment. As a leader or team member, it's essential to recognize the signs of burnout in yourself and others and to create a culture that values well-being as much as productivity.

1. *Foster Open Communication.* Make sure there are open lines of communication between church staff and leadership. Staff members should feel comfortable sharing when they're feeling overwhelmed or when they need additional support. Encourage a culture where asking for help is seen as a strength,

not a weakness, and where leadership is proactive in addressing concerns before they lead to burnout.

2. *Balance Work and Personal Life.* As mentioned in earlier chapters, balancing work and personal life is critical for long-term sustainability in ministry. Make sure staff members are encouraged to take time for themselves and their families and be clear about boundaries between work and personal time. A healthy work-life balance is essential for thriving in ministry and avoiding burnout.

3. *Celebrate Successes and Milestones.* Ministry can often feel like a never-ending list of tasks, but it's important to celebrate successes along the way. Whether it's a successful outreach event, a positive change in someone's life, or simply completing a big project, taking time to celebrate accomplishments helps maintain morale and reminds staff of the impact their work is having.

CARLIE'S STORY—HOW IT COULD HAVE BEEN DIFFERENT

Looking back at Carlie's story, I wonder how things might have been different if we had taken more intentional steps to help her thrive. What if we had built in more support for her early on? What if we had recognized the signs of burnout sooner and intervened with more rest and care? Carlie was an incredible asset to the church, and with the right environment, she could have continued to flourish in her role.

For anyone considering a church staff role, or currently serving in one, the key to thriving is to stay connected to your purpose, prioritize your well-being, and seek support from others. The work you do is incredibly valuable, and when you thrive, the entire church community thrives with you.

FINAL THOUGHTS

Working on church staff can be one of the most rewarding and fulfilling roles you'll ever have. You're part of something bigger than yourself—the redemptive plan of God through His local church. As a member of the supporting cast, you may not always be in the spotlight, but your role is essential to the success of the entire mission.

Remember, your work matters, and so do you. Take the time to care for yourself, stay connected to your calling, and build relationships with those around you. When you do, you'll not only survive the demands of ministry, but you'll thrive—keeping the light in your eyes shining brightly for years to come.

REFLECTION QUESTIONS

1. What steps can you take to stay connected to your original sense of calling in ministry?

2. How can you prioritize rest and renewal in your current church staff role?

3. What support systems do you need to thrive in your kingdom assignment?

MENTOR MOMENTS FOR CHAPTER 17
THRIVING IN YOUR KINGDOM ASSIGNMENT

Objective—Encourage the new staff member to embrace their role as a unique part of God's kingdom work, focusing on ways to grow, find joy, and thrive in their ministry.

Session Title—Embracing the Calling: Finding Joy and Purpose in Ministry

Time Required—30–45 minutes

UNDERSTANDING THE SIGNIFICANCE OF YOUR CALLING

- **Mentor's Prompt**—"Every role in ministry is part of a larger calling. Embracing this calling means recognizing your unique contribution to God's work. Let's discuss what this means for you and how you can find joy in serving."

- **Questions to Consider**
  - How does your role align with your sense of purpose and calling?
  - What aspects of this work bring you the most fulfillment?

NOTES

GROWING IN YOUR ROLE AND SEEKING EXCELLENCE

- **Mentor's Insight**—"Thriving in ministry requires a commitment to personal growth and excellence. Let's talk about ways you can continue growing, both spiritually and professionally, in your role."

- **Questions for Reflection**
  - ° What are some goals you'd like to set for personal or professional growth in this role?
  - ° How can you continue learning and developing your skills to serve effectively?

NOTES

FINDING JOY AND BALANCE IN MINISTRY

- **Mentor's Guidance**—"Ministry can be challenging, but it's also deeply rewarding. Finding joy in serving helps you stay motivated and resilient. Let's discuss ways to maintain a joyful heart in your work, even when challenges arise."
- **Discussion Points**
  - ° What practices or habits help you stay connected to joy and purpose in your work?
  - ° How can you celebrate small victories and moments of impact in your ministry?

NOTES

FINAL REFLECTION AND PRAYER

- **Mentor's Closing Thought**—"Thriving in your kingdom assignment is a journey of growth, joy, and dedication. Take a moment to pray for continued purpose, joy, and strength in this important role."

- **Closing Prayer**—"Lord, thank You for calling [staff member's name] to this assignment. Help them to thrive in their work, finding joy, strength, and purpose each day. May they grow closer to You and inspire others through their service. In Jesus' name, Amen."

APPENDIX

HELPFUL RESOURCES FOR CHURCH STAFF DEVELOPMENT

As you navigate your journey in church staff ministry, here are some valuable resources to help you develop your skills, stay informed, and assess your strengths and gifts. These tools and websites can offer insights into church staff compensation, research on trends in ministry, and assessments to better understand your unique wiring for ministry work.

1. *Vanderbloemen Search Group—Salary and Church Leadership Resources*

   Vanderbloemen is a leading executive search firm specializing in church staffing and leadership. Their 2024 Church Compensation Report provides valuable data on church salaries, benefits, and trends across various roles and church sizes.

   Website: www.vanderbloemen.com

2. *Barna Research Group—Church Trends and Cultural Insights*

   Barna Group is a research organization that provides in-depth studies on faith, culture, leadership, and church trends. Their work is particularly helpful for understanding the challenges and opportunities facing churches in the modern world.

Website: www.barna.com

3. *Pew Research Center—Religion and Public Life Research*

   Pew Research Center is a nonpartisan research organization that offers detailed data on religion, church attendance, and societal trends affecting faith communities. Their research can help church staff understand broader trends and shifts in religious practices and beliefs.

   Website: www.pewresearch.org/religion

4. *Church Unfiltered Podcast—Leadership and Ministry Insights*

   Hosted by Dr. Anthony Cobbs, the Church Unfiltered Podcast addresses key issues facing church leaders and staff. Each episode provides practical wisdom, real-life stories, and insights to help church staff thrive in their ministry roles.

   Website: www.anthonycobbs.com/podcast

5. *Gallup Strengths Assessment—Discovering Your Strengths*

   The Gallup Strengths Assessment helps individuals identify their top strengths and learn how to use them effectively in their roles. As a Gallup-certified coach, I highly recommend this assessment to help church staff understand their unique wiring for ministry.

   Website: www.gallup.com/cliftonstrengths

6. *DISC Personality Assessment—Understanding Behavioral Styles*

   The DISC Assessment is a widely-used tool that helps individuals understand their behavioral tendencies and how to work well with others. It's a helpful resource for church staff looking to improve teamwork and communication within their teams.

   Website: www.discprofile.com

7. *Spiritual Gifts Assessment—Discovering Your God-Given Gifts*

   A Spiritual Gifts Assessment helps individuals discern the spiritual gifts they've been given and how to use them to serve the church effectively. Many churches offer these assessments as part of their ministry development programs.

   Website: www.spiritualgiftstest.com

8. *Personal Website—Anthony Cobbs*

   For more insights, resources, and to connect with me for coaching or speaking engagements, visit my personal website. There, you can also find additional resources related to church staff ministry and leadership development.

   Website: www.anthonycobbs.com

These resources are designed to equip you with the knowledge, insights, and tools needed to thrive in your church staff role. Make use of these assessments and research to enhance your personal growth and contribute more effectively to your church's mission.

www.ingramcontent.com/pod-product-compliance
Lightning Source LLC
Chambersburg PA
CBHW072025060426
42449CB00035B/2597